PREPPER'S
PANTRY

PREPPER'S PANTRY

**Build a Nutritious Stockpile to Survive
Blizzards, Blackouts, Hurricanes, Pandemics,
Economic Collapse, or Any Other Disasters**

Daisy Luther

Racehorse Publishing

Racehorse Publishing books may be purchased in bulk at special discounts for sales promotion, corporate gifts, fund-raising, or educational purposes. Special editions can also be created to specifications. For details, contact the Special Sales Department, Skyhorse Publishing, 307 West 36th Street, 11th Floor, New York, NY 10018 or info@skyhorsepublishing.com.

Racehorse Publishing™ is a pending trademark of Skyhorse Publishing, Inc.®, a Delaware corporation.

Visit our website at www.skyhorsepublishing.com.

10 9 8 7 6 5

Library of Congress Cataloging-in-Publication Data

Names: Luther, Daisy, author.
Title: Prepper's pantry: how to build a nutritious stockpile for disaster
    survival on a budget / by Daisy Luther.
Description: New York, NY: Skyhorse Publishing, [2019]
Identifiers: LCCN 2019002026| ISBN 9781631583919 (pbk.: alk. paper) | ISBN
    9781631583940 (Ebook)
Subjects: LCSH: Grocery shopping. | Food—Storage. | Low budget cooking. |
    Survival and emergency rations.
Classification: LCC TX356 .L88 2019 | DDC 641.3/1—dc23 LC record available
at https://lccn.loc.gov/2019002026

Cover design by Peter Donahue
Cover photos by iStockphoto

Print ISBN: 978-1-63158-391-9
Ebook ISBN: 978-1-63158-394-0

Printed in China

CONTENTS

INTRODUCTION

If you're brand new to prepping, one of the most overwhelming tasks you have ahead of you is building a survival stockpile from scratch. I mean, that is a WHOLE LOT OF FOOD folks are talking about in the forums, am I right?

And building a pantry isn't just for beginners.

Did you ever stop to think about what you would do if all of your preps were gone? Heaven forbid such a misfortune might happen, but what if your pantry was wiped out in a fire or flood? If you had to start over, how would you go about it?

A few years ago, my daughter and I moved across the continent, from the easternmost part of Ontario to the Pacific Northwest of the US. Because we were crossing the border, driving through extreme heat, and then storing our belongings in a trailer for a month, we couldn't bring our food supplies. We still had our tools and equipment, but we started over as far as our pantry was concerned. And, we only brought a small trailer, so we also started from scratch for goods like toilet paper and laundry soap.

Being without my one-year supply of food made me feel uncomfortable and very vulnerable, given the circumstances in the world today.

I thought it might be interesting, especially to new preppers, to show you how we rebuilt our food supply on a very tight budget. (That move was expensive!)

So, with that in mind, I wrote *The Pantry Primer* in 2013 to document our journey, and published it in 2014.

That book was based on my blog posts about our fresh start, but the reviews and emails I received from the readers let me know that you wanted a lot more information than I initially provided. So, because of that, I revised and nearly tripled it in size. And now, I have been given the opportunity to revamp yet again with this newest and most updated edition!

This book is geared towards people who are just starting out on their preparedness journey. Even if you've been at it for a while, you'll still find some creative ideas for shopping on a budget. That being said, you may find that some of the concepts discussed are things that you already know—you may want to skip forward to Part 2. I hope that you'll still find the how-to information valuable, and maybe you can "pay it forward" by taking the time to advise someone less experienced.

In each section, we'll discuss two things: *Why* and *How.*

While knowing *how* to do something is of vital importance, I always find that I personally learn much better if I also know *why* I'm doing it in that particular way. Some of the information is based on history, and some of it is based on my personal experiences.

So, let's get started. We have a lot of work to do, but don't worry! I'll walk you through it every step of the way.

Part I
WHY YOU NEED A FOOD STORAGE PANTRY

Why Do You Need a One-Year Food Supply?

A year's supply of food.

Does that sound like a ridiculous amount? Why on earth would you need a one-year food supply? There are four grocery stores in your town, not to mention Walmart and Target. Food is EVERYWHERE!

Simple: A one-year food supply means freedom. It means that you are less subject to the whims of the economy. You can handle small disasters with aplomb. You aren't reliant on the government if a crisis strikes.

Below I've listed some reasons why a food supply is important.

Personal Financial Disasters

People often ask me how I got started prepping. Nearly everyone who is into this lifestyle has a notable incident that made them pause and think, *Hmm . . . I need to do things differently.*

For me, there were two incidents that made an enormous, life-altering impression.

A *long* time ago, when I was newly married and in my early 20s, my husband and I welcomed a beautiful baby girl who turned our world upside down. Suddenly, we weren't just a young couple who could get by on only a few dollars until the next paycheck arrived. We had real responsibilities, and we needed to take life more seriously.

When our little bundle was just a month old, I had begun doing just that. I had planted a nice big vegetable garden in the yard of our rented home, and I'd taken advantage of a good sale and put a dozen packages of bagels in our freezer and several jars of peanut butter in our pantry.

That was the same day that my husband came home, white-faced, to tell me he had been laid off.

Panic didn't ensue immediately. We had his last check and the week's groceries. We knew he'd qualify for unemployment, since he'd paid into that fund for a sufficient amount of time. He was young, strong, and hardworking, we reasoned, so he'd have a new job in no time at all.

Unfortunately, it soon became clear that there were few jobs to be had in our depressed area. Unemployment checks were eight long weeks away. Soon, we were broke and had nothing but the bagels and peanut butter, and some hopes for our garden.

It took five months before my husband found a job, and those were lean months indeed. But I had learned an incredibly valuable lesson: Stock up now, because you never know what tomorrow might bring. When we finally had some money coming in, I began to shop the sales diligently, organizing grocery trips with the ruthlessness of an invading army. Even on the miniscule amount of money we received from the unemployment office, I managed to put back a week's worth of extra food, then a month's worth, then even more.

That was the beginning of my preparedness lifestyle, even though I had absolutely no idea what prepping was at the time.

The next incident took ten years to occur, but this was the one that solidified things for me. Throughout the years, I had continued to stock my pantry, shopping the sales, and putting things back as I could. By this time, another lovely little girl had been born, and I was the single mom of two. I had a decent job in the automotive industry, but there wasn't a lot of extra money. I'd bought a tiny little house with a tiny little yard and was busting my rear to build some stability for my daughters.

Then, just like my husband had before, I got laid off in a mass culling of my former workplace.

Suddenly, I was without income. Here I was with a mortgage payment, a car payment, and all the assorted expenses that come with homes and cars. I had two children to support, and no money coming in.

But this time it was different.

Totally, completely different.

Sure, it is always scary to lose your income source, but I had a safety net sitting there in the back room of my house.

That safety net wasn't soft and squishy. It was made of cans, boxes, and buckets. We had enough food to get us through at least 6 months of not buying a darned thing. This meant that my limited money could pay the bills to keep a car in the driveway and a roof over our head.

And for me, this sealed the deal. While other friends who had been laid off at the same time were struggling, we were just fine. In fact, we were able to help some of them out with groceries right out of our pantry and freezer.

In an uncertain economic climate, we never know when a personal crisis might befall us. Whether it's the loss of a job, a large unexpected medical bill, or just an increase in expenses without an increase in pay, a sudden financial problem can happen to anyone. Building a pantry means that your bills can still get paid while your family is fed. And this, my friends, is the best insurance you can buy.

Short-Term Local Disasters

I can think of a dozen short-term disasters that have happened over the past few years right here in America that left people without access to stores for a few days up to a few weeks. For some of these incidents, there was a little bit of advance warning, but when everyone is getting the same warning, it doesn't take long for the shelves to be stripped bare. If you already have your supplies, you have no need to go out and fight the crowd beforehand, nor do you have to make a potentially risky trip to get supplies in the aftermath of the disaster.

Here are two examples of localized issues that will put your stockpile to use:

Storms: Winter storms or hurricanes, depending on your geographic location, will keep you stranded at home. If the power goes out on top of it, you will need not only cooking ingredients, but a stash of foods that do not require lengthy (or any) cooking time, since your ability to use the stove may also be impaired by the outage. Some examples of this are Superstorm Sandy, which battered the Eastern Seaboard a few years ago, and the hurricanes that head for the Gulf of Mexico and the states next to it nearly every year.

Civil unrest: The situation in the small town Ferguson, Missouri, a few years back kept people trapped in their homes for a week at a time on two separate occasions. An unpopular verdict after a police shooting escalated racial tensions, and rioters rampaged through the small town. Stores closed to try and prevent being looted, and local residents were forced to make do with the supplies they had on hand.

In either of the above situations, your pantry will be the difference between being able to stay safely at home or being forced to go out and brave the situation with many other desperate people.

A Short History Lesson about Liberty

Finally, food is freedom. Your supplies are more than just supplies. The stockpile in your pantry is the key to your independence.

Food is a control mechanism and has been for centuries. Throughout history, groups of people have been literally starved into submission when the government took over food production. In each case, you will see that the government started out by controlling how the food was grown.

- In 1932–33, the Ukraine, formerly the breadbasket of Russia, was turned into a desolate wasteland during the Holodomor. Malcolm Muggeridge wrote in his book, *War on the Peasants*, "On one side, millions of starving peasants, their bellies often swollen from lack of food; on the other, soldiers, members of the GPU (secret police) carrying out the instructions of the dictatorship of the proletariat. They had gone over the country like a swarm of locusts and taken away everything edible, they had shot or exiled thousands of peasants, sometimes whole villages, they had reduced some of the most fertile land in the world to a melancholy desert." More than 7 million people died so that their farms could be collectivized by Moscow.

- The Hunger Plan, an economic management system created by the sick mind of Herbert Backe, caused the deaths of 4.2 million people in German-occupied territories of the Soviet Union. The Hunger Plan diverted food from the citizens of the occupied territories and used it to feed the German military. In a meeting the Nazi State leaders concluded, "The war can only be continued if the entire Wehrmacht is fed from Russia in the third year of the war. If we take what we need out of the country, there can be no doubt that tens of millions of people will die of starvation. . . . Many tens of millions of people in this country will become superfluous and will die or must emigrate to Siberia. Attempts to rescue the population there from death through starvation by obtaining surpluses from the black earth zone . . . prevent the possibility of Germany holding out till the end of the war." Rations allowed by the Germans for many people in the subjugated areas were *less than 200 calories per day*. The citizens were forced to work the farms, from which they were not allowed harvests, in return for those meager rations.

- The policies of the Communist Party in China caused more than 76 million people to starve between the years 1958 and 1961. Called the Three Years of Great Chinese Famine, the government had ruled that changes in farming techniques were the law. People were not allowed private plots to grow their own food and all farms were arranged into communes (collectivism strikes again). Yang Jisheng, a Chinese historian, wrote in his book *Tombstone*, "In Xinyang, people starved at the doors of the grain warehouses. As they died, they shouted, 'Communist Party, Chairman Mao, save us.' If the granaries of Henan and Hebei had been opened, no one need have died. As people were dying in large numbers around them, officials did not think to save them. Their only concern was how to fulfill the delivery of grain." To this day, Yang Jisheng's book about the famine is banned on mainland China.

There are many more examples of starvation as a control mechanism throughout history—but the key point is that it has happened before and, to paraphrase an old saying, those who don't learn from history are doomed to repeat it.

And Here We Are . . .

So, here we are, just like at other times in history, right on the verge of an economic crisis and increasing losses of freedom.

This is the part that some people don't want to read—the part that makes preparedness "controversial."

It's no conspiracy theory to state that our economy is shaky, our Bill of Rights is under constant attack, and our country is incredibly

divided. The offerings at the grocery stores are not just poor, they're toxic, but growing your own food is sometimes frowned upon and definitely made difficult in many parts of the country.

We are being spied on, taxed, legislated, and silenced. We've become a nation of consumers instead of a nation of producers and that is incredibly dangerous. It's dangerous because it gives all the power to the producers, and it's dangerous because many old-fashioned skills and philosophies are on the verge of being lost.

But you can protect your family and provide them with stability, simply by being self-reliant. And that starts with a pantry full of food.

The Plan

When I wrote my first book, the goal for us was to rebuild a healthy one-year food supply over the course of three months, using the following methods:

- Shopping the sales
- Buying in bulk
- Buying from local farmers and preserving the harvest
- Getting a fall garden going

Our budget wasn't big. We started at square one—our cupboards were absolutely empty.

Our journey was comparable to that of a family with a week-to-week budget who is just beginning to build a pantry.

Because we were concurrently shopping for groceries we'd be eating immediately and all of those odds and ends which arise when you move into a new home, I wasn't able to blow an entire week's grocery money on a 100-pound bag of sugar and a 100-pound bag of wheat berries—I had to also keep us fed, healthy, and in clean clothing.

The bigger purchases came after a few weeks of building the pantry, when I was able to forgo a weekly shopping trip and put that money towards some large purchases.

What You'll Learn

We're going to talk about food storage from beginning to end. We'll talk about the components of a pantry, in-depth. We'll discuss a new way to shop that helps you get the most bang from your bucks. We will go week-by-week creating a stockpile. The amounts are up to you and your budget. Simply repeat steps until you have everything you need. And then, we'll discuss what to do with all of that food: how to store it, where to store it, and how to manage your inventory so you can eat from this food and still maintain a one-year supply.

If You're New to This . . .

Please don't be discouraged when you see all the doom and gloom out there. You can take the most important step today—the step of getting started. You'll have a year's supply of food in no time at all!

Part II
ALL ABOUT THE PERFECT PANTRY

In every relationship there comes a time when you must sit down and take a serious look at the future. Where do you want to go? Are your goals compatible? Are things working as they stand right now or do some changes need to be made?

Your pantry is no different. People create food storage stockpiles for many different reasons, and because of this, there is no "one-size-fits-all" formula for doing so. You must figure out what your goals are and develop a road map towards achieving them.

In this section, we'll talk about your food supply: how much food you need, the types of pantry-building styles, why storing the healthiest food possible is important, a pantry break-down by specific components, and special considerations for family members who have dietary restrictions.

Figuring Out How Much You Need

The first step is figuring out how much food your family would need to have for a one-year supply.

You probably won't be anywhere near a one-year food supply if you haven't been putting forth some diligent effort, but don't worry about that. These calculations will give you something to shoot for.

There are several resources online for food calculators. The Latter Day Saints website, ProvidentLiving.com, has one of the most popular ones, but there are others, too. Don't worry too much about which one you use because this is just a general starting point.

Based on a consensus among several different food calculators, the following amounts are an annual supply for one family member over the age of 7.

- Grains: 300 pounds
- Beans: 60 pounds
- Dry milk: 75 pounds
- Sugars: 60 pounds
- Fats: 15 pounds
- Fruits and vegetables: 1500 servings (combination of dried, canned, and fresh)

None of the food storage calculators seem to have much information on protein aside from beans, but rest assured, there are many other options.

I know that seems like a vast amount of food (and it's only for ONE person). Don't be overwhelmed! In upcoming chapters, we'll discuss exactly how to make it happen, even on a budget. Not only will you create your stockpile, you'll learn to shop in a new way that will save you piles of money on your grocery bill over the course of a year.

Two Important Notes about Your Pantry

First of all, I want to strongly encourage you to build your pantry to reflect your current eating habits. When disaster strikes, familiarity is very comforting. Particularly if you have children, you don't want to suddenly begin serving them food that is completely outside of their normal diet. They will likely rebel and refuse to eat it, and during a crisis, you don't want to see food go to waste.

The other reason for keeping your pantry as close to your regular diet as possible is that suddenly switching the foods you eat will cause serious gastrointestinal upset for many people. This doesn't just apply to those with dietary restrictions. For example, many people these days don't consume grains often at all. They eat mostly protein, fats, and vegetables. A sudden switch to a steady intake of beans and rice would have those folks rushing to the bathroom for days. You'll have enough to deal with during a crisis without adding preventable illness.

Secondly, it's very important to remember that once you *think* you have a one-year food supply, you should continue to build your pantry. Disasters don't go by the books, and no formula can tell you how much you will need to eat. Stress increases your need for calories, and epic events are nothing if not stressful. Furthermore, you may be doing a lot more physical labor to produce food and repair structures, which will also increase your caloric need. A supply that would last for a year during non-eventful times will probably *not* stretch that far if you are completely reliant on your pantry.

Your Pantry Is Directly Related to Your Health

Since I'm "The Organic Prepper" you probably knew that I'd be talking about building your pantry in a healthful way. You were right. So, let's talk about this before we go any further, so that it's clear why some of the recommendations I'll be making are *not* the absolute least expensive options.

It would be easy to slip into the mindset of rapidly buying any food you could get your hands on cheaply in order to create your stockpile quickly. Lots of people do it, putting back hundreds of packages of ramen noodles and beef stew with "formed chunks." This is not the way you want to go about it, particularly if your day-to-day menu is healthy.

Obviously, a certain amount of processing is necessary to preserve the food for a year, but always opt for the least-processed items with the fewest ingredients. Buy the best quality of food that you can afford.

Here's why: In the midst of a crisis, it is especially vital to be well-nourished. You may be calling upon your body to perform a lot more physical activity than you do in your day-to-day life at an office job, and you'll need fuel for that. Many people become ill during times of crisis. In any stressful situation, whether it's a personal economic crisis or an epic natural disaster that has struck your area, your immune system takes a beating. You don't want your body to have to fight off the effects of toxic food at the same time.

You want the food you put into your body to be the kind of food that strengthens your immune system, provides energy, and keeps you healthy.

If you are in a situation where you have a family to feed and don't have a lot of money to do it, you need to do your research well before looking at those brightly colored packages with the false promises of nutrition within.

While this list isn't comprehensive, here are some things to consider about conventional grocery store offerings.

GMOs: Genetically modified foods have not been tested for long-term effects on humans. There is some evidence to indicate the GMOs can cause a host of illness. It's up to you whether or not you wish to include genetically modified foods in your pantry. If you *are* avoiding them, you should note that nearly all of the corn and soy sold in the United States is GMO, so those are two ingredients to avoid purchasing non-organic if you want to keep genetically modified organisms out of your pantry.

Hormones and antibiotics: Livestock animals that provide meat or dairy products are tainted with growth hormones, antibiotics, and GMO feed. These items pass through the food chain to the consumer. Growth hormones can cause opposite sex characteristics in developing children, early puberty, the development of cancer, and infertility. Furthermore, the world is quickly becoming immune to the effects of antibiotics because of constant exposure through the food supply, which means that there is the potential for things that should be easily treated to become deadly due to antibiotic resistance.

Pesticides: The use of pesticides in conventional farming is rampant. Even the hijacked Environmental Protection Agency has to admit that the ingestion of pesticides can cause health problems. They warn of the risk of "birth defects, nerve damage, cancer, and other effects that might occur over a long period of time." (Keep in mind, however, that despite this warning, the EPA just *raised* the acceptable limit of glyphosate.) Especially at risk of harm from pesticides are prepubescent children and fetuses.

Neurotoxins: Our water supply is spiked with fluoride, which is a neurotoxin that lowers IQs, causes infertility, has been linked to cancer, and causes hardening of the arteries. Nearly every packaged food on the shelf is seasoned with MSG in one of its many names. MSG is a "flavor enhancer" that is used to make cheap, low-quality ingredients taste better. Many lower-calorie foods and diet drinks that tout their "health benefits" are sweetened with aspartame. Both of these are excitotoxins that cause brain cell death instantly, and can cause decreased IQs, headaches (migraines in some particularly sensitive people), depression, anxiety, and seizures.

Assorted chemical cocktails: The length of the ingredients list in your food is often a direct indicator of the unhealthiness of the item. When an item contains a host of additives, colors, flavors, and preservatives, you can safely bet that most of the nutrients are gone. These highly processed food-like substances are very difficult for the body to break down so that the few remaining nutrients can be used.

If you can't picture what an ingredient looked like in its natural state, it probably isn't something you really want to eat. When is the last time you saw a tertiary butyl hydroquinone grazing in a field, or a calcium propionate growing in the garden?

What Should You Should Eat When You're Broke?

Let's face it, nearly everyone would like to eat a perfect diet of organic produce, grass-fed, humanely-raised meat, and hormone-free dairy products. Of course, we'd also like a personal chef with that, and a summer home on the beach. Alas, reality interferes with those dreams for most of us.

Sometimes it just isn't financially feasible to stick to your usual restrictions. It is a matter, then, of weighing the pros and cons, and figuring out what things, for you, are the most important, while also deciding which standards can be sacrificed. These decisions will be different for everyone, based on their personal health concerns, their genetic propensity for certain diseases, and the members of the family for whom they are buying the food.

Sometimes, when you're looking at someone else's situation while you are comfortably backed by a loaded pantry, it's easy to be judgmental and tell them what they "should" do. The thing that we must all remember is that when times are tough, a person may be down to these two options with a two-week grocery budget:

1) **Buy strictly healthy organic foods and feed your family for perhaps 8 out of the 14 days.**
2) **Carefully select which standards you will relax to keep the tummies of your family full throughout the wait for the next paycheck.**

Very few people are going to choose option one. It just doesn't make sense.

When your budget is tight, here are some things to consider.

Grains: If you can't swing organic grains, look for whole grains with few or no additives.

- Wheat flour
- Brown rice (We always opt for rice grown in the US. The cheap rice from China is often held to very low standards, bereft of nutrition, and highly chemically treated.)
- Pasta (with recognizable ingredients)
- Couscous
- Quinoa
- Barley

Fruits and vegetables: If organic produce is not an option, look for the items with the lowest pesticide loads. Fruits and vegetables that can be peeled often subject you to fewer pesticides than thin-skinned items.

If you must buy conventional, wash the produce carefully and peel it if possible. Look to these standbys:

- Apples (peeled)
- Asparagus
- Avocados
- Cabbage
- Cantaloupe
- Eggplant
- Grapefruit
- Kiwi
- Mangoes
- Mushrooms
- Onions
- Oranges
- Pineapples
- Rutabagas
- Sweet Peas
- Sweet Potatoes
- Turnips

Dairy products: Conventional dairy products are absolutely loaded with hormones. Dairy cattle are given high levels of female hormones to make them produce a greater quantity of milk. This can cause little boys to develop female characteristics and little girls to hit puberty at a far younger age than normal, which is sometimes the reason you see 4th graders with large breasts and hips. These hormones can also trigger obesity in both genders. Because of the public outcry, some dairies have pledged not to use rBST, the most commonly used of the growth hormones. Do your research to discover if there are any such brands available to you.

It's interesting to note that the FDA forces those who label their products rBST-free to also put the following disclaimer on the containers: "No significant difference has been shown between milk derived from rBST-treated and non-rBST-treated cows."

Organic dairy is still better, because the cattle are generally

fed a healthier diet and are free from antibiotics. If you can't swing it, at the very least, search for rBST-free dairy products. For other products, you can save loads of money by making your own from untainted milk. Learn how to make yogurt, how to make yogurt cheese, and how to make cottage cheese. These things are all so easy you'll wonder why you hadn't been making them all along. Plain yogurt can also be used as a healthy substitute for sour cream.

Water: If you are on city water, chances are, your water is loaded with chemicals, from fluoride to ammonia to chlorine. I won't drink this water, and I won't let my children drink it either. The large 5-gallon jugs provide the least expensive way to buy water. You can also look for sources of spring water to fill your own containers. Putting your tap water through a high quality water filtration device that removes fluoride is another option.

The Components of a Perfect Pantry

The perfect pantry will meet all of your nutritional needs. It will provide the ingredients you need for energy, for repairing muscles and tissues, for fighting off illness and disease, and for maintaining a healthy body weight.

The perfect pantry will also supply you with the odds and ends necessary for scratch cooking, which is the healthiest and most frugal way to cook.

In this section we'll talk about the building blocks of your pantry: grains, protein, fruits and vegetables, and scratch-cooking basics.

Grains

As I mentioned above, most food storage calculators recommend 300 pounds of grains *per person* for a one-year supply. For a family of four, that is a whopping 1200 pounds of food in *just this one category* that you should store if you are trying to build a one-year pantry!

That sounds like a really daunting number until you remember that it is divided over many different items. To name a few:

- Rice
- Flour
- Wheat

- Quinoa
- Couscous
- Cornmeal

- Barley
- Oats
- Pasta

Divide up your grain storage based on your family's preferences. After all, if only one person likes rice, the rest of you won't want to be stuck having it at every other meal if you must live off your stockpile for a year.

Most grains can be purchased in very large quantities at greatly reduced prices. Amazon has a good variety of bulk organic grains that can be delivered to your door.

When purchasing items in amounts over 20 pounds, your food storage methods become particularly important. To decide what storage methods you should use, you must ask yourself whether you intend for these goods to be your long-term food storage, remaining untouched unless disaster strikes, or whether you intend to rotate them from the pantry to the kitchen, using them and replenishing your pantry as needed. There is detailed information on food storage methods beginning on page 121.

For now, let's take a closer look at these essential pantry building blocks.

Rice

More than 3 billion people across the world eat rice every day. Rice has long been at the top of the hierarchy in the prepper's pantry. It's inexpensive, a source of energy-boosting carbohydrates, and can extend one humble serving of meat into a meal for an entire hungry family.

Conventionally grown rice has a very high pesticide load. PANNA (Pesticide Action Network of North America) identified more than 40 different pesticides on rice grown in California, with 15 of those pesticides on their "bad actors" list—which means that the pesticides have been proven in multiple studies to have negative effects on human beings and/or groundwater systems.

The website "What's on My Food?"* noted that the pesticides included those which were known to be carcinogenic, bee toxins,

---

*http://www.whatsonmyfood.org/food.jsp?food=RI.

human reproductive and developmental toxins, neurotoxins, and suspected hormone disruptors.

Rice that has been grown organically is not soaked in pesticides and fungicides from seed to package, like conventional rice. This is a vast improvement for the purity and nutritional value of a bulk rice purchase. White rice, when stored properly, has a far longer shelf life than brown rice, which is far more nutritious (and many find it much tastier as well).

Unfortunately, though, even organic rice is not the best thing to serve on a regular basis. Recent studies have shown that all rice, organic and conventional, has a high level of naturally occurring arsenic.

Arsenic is a metallic element that is toxic to multi-cellular life forms. There are two types of arsenic: inorganic and organic. Inorganic arsenic has not bonded with carbon, and is a known carcinogen. Organic arsenic is found in seafood and is generally considered to be non-toxic. It is excreted through urine within about 48 hours of consumption.

Arsenic is taken into the rice from the soil, through the roots of the plant. Arsenic can get into the soil in many different ways, including the use of arsenic-containing pesticides. These pesticides can remain in the soil for up to 45 years after they were sprayed. Another source of arsenic in the soil is fertilizer made from chicken droppings—commercial chicken feed has been found to have high levels of the toxin. When rice fields are deliberately flooded, the water-soluble arsenic in the soil is delivered to the roots of the plants.

Brown rice contains more arsenic than white rice—the arsenic accumulates in the hull, which is stripped during processing. The hull, however, contains most of the nutrients in the rice.

Arsenic can be toxic in both the short-term and the long-term. Everyone is familiar with the use of arsenic as a poison.

According to the Mayo Clinic:[*]

"Arsenic is perhaps the best known of the metal toxins, having gained notoriety from its extensive use by Renaissance nobility as an anti-syphilitic agent. . . . A wide range of signs and symptoms may be seen in acute arsenic poisoning including headache, nausea, vomiting, diarrhea, abdominal pain, hypotension, fever, hemolysis, seizures, and mental status changes. Symptoms of chronic poisoning, also called arse-niasis, are mostly insidious and nonspecific. The gastrointestinal tract, skin, and central nervous system are usually involved. Nausea, epigas-tric pain, colic abdominal pain, diarrhea, and paresthesias of the hands and feet can occur."

Rice can still be an important part of your pantry, but it should not be consumed on a daily basis, lest a build-up of this toxic heavy metal occur in your body.

Oats

Oats can be used to add extra fiber to baked goods, in place of breadcrumbs in meatballs and meatloaf, and as a hot cereal. They are also a staple ingredient in granola, and of course, the much beloved oatmeal cookie! Oats can be purchased in bulk quantities and then repackaged for long shelf life.

When oats are grown, they look similar to wheat. Little kernels called "groats" are removed from the hulls and then, most of the time, are minimally processed in a mill to ready them for human consumption.

Oats are milled in several different ways:

- **Whole groats**: These little kernels look similar to rice. They take a very long time to cook, about an hour and a half, so they may not be the best choice for emergency food.

---

[*]http://www.mayomedicallaboratories.com/test-catalog/Clinical +and+Interpretive/8644.

They are the least processed of all of the oat varieties and have a slight nutty flavor. Groats can be used in place of rice or pasta, or as a hot cereal.

- **Steel-cut oats**: Steel cut oats are groats chopped into just a few pieces with (big shock) a steel blade. They take about a half an hour to cook, have a chewier texture than more processed oats, and are known for their more complex flavor.

- **Rolled oats:** Rolled oats are a bit more processed. Groats are steamed to soften then, then rolled into flakes. This process actually stabilizes the naturally-occurring oils in the oats, which makes them more shelf-stable than steel-cut oats or groats. Rolled oats only take about 5 minutes to cook.

- **Quick-cooking oats:** Quick oats are simply rolled oats, but thinner. Because they are thinner, they cook extremely quickly—they can be ready in about 1 minute. This is a definite perk in a down-grid scenario, since you won't have to waste precious fuel during a long cooking time. The downside of quick oats is that they don't maintain their texture as well as rolled or steel-cut oats.

Flour

Very shortly after wheat is cracked open, it loses 60% of its beneficial nutrients. This is the reason many people store wheat berries instead of flour. I do store flour, however, first as a convenience item, and secondly, because the addition of a small amount of commercial flour improves the texture of my homemade bread.

Whole wheat flour has more of the bran, which results in its brownish color. However, the bran contains volatile oils, which can quickly become rancid. Whole wheat flour has a short shelf life.

White flour has the bran removed. I recommend unbleached white flour for storage. It still has the bran removed, but won't be as white as the flour we've grown used to in North America, because it is not chemically processed with bleach.

Wheat

Wheat berries are the "real" whole wheat. Wheat berries are actually not berries at all—they are kernels of wheat. They can be purchased in soft white or hard red wheat berries.

The benefits to wheat berries over flour are numerous: They last almost indefinitely when stored properly; they are a mighty source of nutrients, vitamins, and minerals; and they can be used in a wide variety of ways. You can grind them into flour (be sure you have a hand grinder that will work off-grid). You can also cook them whole and make a yummy pilaf as a side dish or a hot breakfast cereal.

One type of wheat you should consider is einkorn wheat. This is an heirloom variety that is very similar to the unmodified wheat our ancestors consumed. Many people believe that this wheat is less likely to cause issues with gluten intolerance than more modern varieties.

Pasta

This quick and easy comfort food comes in many different shapes and sizes. Whole wheat pasta, while more nutritious, doesn't last as long on the shelf as does white pasta, so let your planned shelf life be a determining factor in which type of noodles you choose to buy. Pasta cooks up very quickly, using little fuel, so it is a good choice as long as you have the resources to boil water. Depending on the shelf life you require, you may not need to repackage pasta to keep it fresh. This is an item that goes on sale frequently, so stock up whenever you can.

You might also consider adding rice noodles to your pasta stash because of their quick preparation time. Simply add boiling water, then cover the noodles and allow them to soften. Within 10 minutes, they're ready to be added to a stir-fry or topped with meat and vegetables.

Quinoa

This delicious little kernel is the highest protein grain around. Quinoa (pronounced keen'-wah) was held sacred by the Incas, who called it the "mother of all grains." This ancient grain has had a recent resurgence in popularity because of its excellent nutritional profile, easy preparation, and versatile nutty taste.

Quinoa is more expensive than most other grains, but the high-quality nutrients make it a great investment. Quinoa contains significant amounts of thiamine, riboflavin, vitamin B6, niacin, vitamin E, and folate, as well as minerals like iron, magnesium, phosphorus, potassium, and zinc.

Quinoa is used as a grain, but is actually a seed that is closely related to beetroot, spinach, and tumbleweeds. Weird, huh? It's actually a *"pseudo grain."* It contains complete protein, including amino acids.

Make sure the quinoa you purchase for your stockpile has been processed to remove the bitter coating (called saponin). In an emergency situation, you don't want to have to use your precious water storage to wash your grains. Not only does the saponin taste terrible, it can also cause gastrointestinal distress.

Cornmeal

I strongly recommend seeking organic options for all things "corn" as more than 80% of corn in North America is genetically modified, making it a questionable choice for your food storage pantry.

I purchase very coarsely ground cornmeal, also known as grits or polenta. You can run this through your grinder to make it finer for baking, or mix it 2:1 with flour.

Barley

This easy-to-cook, very neutral grain is a high-fiber addition to soups, stews, and casseroles. It has a nutty flavor and a similar consistency to pasta. It is sold in different forms: hulled, pearled, flaked, scotch (or pot), or grits.

Barley can be fermented and used in the production of beer or whiskey. Barley contains gluten, so should not be consumed by those with gluten intolerance or celiac disease.

Amaranth

Amaranth is a high-quality protein that is similar to quinoa, so it serves double duty in the pantry. The part of the plant consumed is the seeds. It can be served as a pilaf, ground and used as a baking ingredient, or made into a hot breakfast cereal. It's very gentle on the system and easily digestible, making it a perfect food for someone who is recovering from an illness. It only takes about 20–25 minutes to cook.

Amaranth is very versatile. In Mexico, amaranth seeds are popped like popcorn, and then tossed in honey, chocolate, or molasses. This is sweet treat is called "alegria."

Buckwheat

Despite the name, buckwheat is not actually wheat at all, or even a grain. It's considered biologically to be part of the fruit family and is related to sorrel and rhubarb. The part we consume is the seed, which is dried and ground into a flour substitute.

It doesn't contain gluten, so it won't rise like flour. However, buckwheat makes delightful pancakes that don't require all sorts of gums and magical ingredients and a chant to give them a nice texture like most gluten-free pancakes. Buckwheat can be served as a substitute for rice or as a hot breakfast cereal.

Buckwheat is sold either roasted or unroasted. The roasted variety is called "kasha" in Eastern Europe, where it is traditionally served over pasta, then topped with onions and brown gravy, in a dish called kasha varnishkes. I recommend purchasing the whole buckwheat groats and then grinding them as needed into flour or roasting them lightly.

There are other grains that are more processed that you may add to your pantry:

- Crackers
- Tortillas
- Breakfast cereal
- Instant oatmeal
- Melba toast

These should be eaten in the short-term instead of stashing them away for a year, as the shelf-life isn't extremely long. Only add these to your stockpile if they are part of your normal diet.

Protein

One area in which many pantries are lacking is protein. Because meat is so perishable (and also expensive) it is often the most neglected frontier of the one-year pantry.

This is unfortunate, because protein is a vital addition to your pantry. Without proper protein consumption, hard-working muscles cannot heal and strengthen. Particularly in a disaster situation, you may be called upon to perform much harder physical labor than you are accustomed to. Protein is a necessity to provide your body with the nutrients it needs to repair itself and become stronger. Tess Pennington of ReadyNutrition.com wrote on her website:[*]

---

[*] http://readynutrition.com/resources/the-top-5-protein-sources-for-your-shtf-diet_27032013/

Being well-nourished during a disaster can mean the difference between powering through the event with strength, stamina, and energy, or plodding through the situation barely able to put one foot in front of the other.

One often overlooked component of the prepper's pantry is protein. This vital nutrient:

- *Helps with the repair and building of muscle tissue*
- *Helps the body heal from injuries*
- *Provides long-lasting stamina*
- *Helps boost the immune system*

Protein is stored throughout the body. It can be found in muscles, bones, hemoglobin, myoglobin, hormones, antibodies, and enzymes. In fact, protein makes up nearly 45% of the human body. Without a steady supply, body functions will cease to operate effectively.

Take heart. You don't have to be relegated to those nasty cans of minced up chicken parts or tins of fish. There are several strategies you can use to stockpile protein and still feed your family healthy food during rough times.

Go vegetarian

Wait! Don't throw the book away! You don't have to go totally vegetarian to use this strategy.

An occasional meatless meal will stretch your budget and extend your meat supply.

Add the following healthy vegetarian protein sources to your pantry:

- **Dried beans:** When well-packed, dried beans can last up to 10 years. Beans can also be sprouted to provide a quick source of fresh veggies in a longer-term emergency.
- **Canned beans:** Some emergencies mean that your normal method of cooking may not be available. If the power grid is down, canned beans (whether purchased at the store or home-canned) will provide instant protein in the blink of an eye.

- **Quinoa:** This little grain is a nutritional powerhouse and contains 8 grams of protein per cup. (Learn more about quinoa in the previous section on grains.)
- **Nuts and nut butters:** Shelf life for nut products is shorter because the fats can go rancid— plan for about a one-year shelf life.
- **Texturized vegetable protein:** Beware: more than 80% of the soy sold in North America is genetically modified. (So your tofu, soy sauce, soy milk, and food additives like hydrolyzed soy protein are probably GMO unless they're organic.) Only purchase ORGANIC TVP if you wish to avoid GMOs, the consumption of which many studies say can be detrimental to human health.

Protein Powder

Protein powder isn't just for bodybuilders. It can be a great addition to your prepper stockpile (or even to your diet right now!).

A lot of folks aren't getting enough protein for good health. If we ate the 10 servings of fruits and vegetables that are recommended along with a sufficient amount of protein, we'd be eating almost constantly. But we often end up reaching for unhealthy snacks to fill us up that do nothing to meet our nutritional needs.

A good quality protein powder can turn a "snack" into a nutritional motherlode at the touch of a blender. In fact, you don't even have to have a blender if all you want is the protein part. There are shaker cups with a little whisk ball inside that will thoroughly mix most good protein powders with nothing but people power. (I like the ones with at least 28 ounces for more shaker space.)

It can also play a part if you have a family member who isn't eating for some reason. Perhaps they're sick and maybe they just don't have an appetite due to the stress of the situation. A shake loaded with protein powder, nutrient-rich fruits, and a base of milk (dairy or non-dairy), can provide everything a person needs with no chewing required.

Some powders have additional vitamins and minerals added in, or you can also get vitamin powders to go into your shake. A green superfood powder adds the goodness of fruits and vegetables on the go (perfect for an emergency) and liquid trace minerals are also available. You can also add a dropper of any type of herbal tincture that you happen to be taking.

An unopened tub of protein powder lasts for about two years, so this isn't something to plop in the bunker for decades. It should be rotated into your kitchen pantry and enjoyed now, just like any other shorter-term product.

Protein powder is one of the few things that is best stored in the package it comes in. (Assuming it comes in one of those plastic canisters with a sealed inner top.) If it comes in a bag, you may want to put that bag into another mylar bag, but avoid opening the original bag until you're ready to use it. Exposure to oxygen is the kiss of death for a longer-term freshness for this product. Keep it in a cool, dry, dark place.

All protein powders are not created equally. Some of the ones with garish colors and outlandish claims are nothing but chemical bombs and should be strictly avoided. I also avoid any products that contain soy. The higher quality ones are more expensive but very worthwhile.

My very favorite brand is Naked. It is free of additives and is nothing but pure, clean ingredients. At first glance, the product seems outrageously expensive, but this is because it only comes in larger sizes (like 5 pounds). However, if you're going to use it, per serving, it works out to a lower price than most high-quality products at only $1.11 per serving.

Naked is available in many varieties for nearly any dietary need. They have powders with whey, rice, pea, peanut butter, and goat milk proteins.

When looking for a protein powder, I check the following:

How is it sweetened? If it's with aspartame or sucralose, pass it by. A natural cane sugar is better than something artificial, but coconut sugar or stevia are the best choices.

Where does the protein come from? If you are lactose intolerant, of course, a whey or casein protein will be bad news for you. Hemp protein has an earthy flavor some people strongly dislike in a fruity shake, but the unflavored one isn't bad in a savory dish. Pea protein and egg protein are very light-tasting. This is all based on your personal preference.

Does it have a bunch of extra ingredients promising exaggerated benefits? If those ingredients are completely unidentifiable, you may want to pass this one over. The idea here is to boost your nutrition, not to drink the equivalent of vanilla Doritos.

How much protein does one serving contain? Ideally, you want a product that contains 15 grams of protein at the minimum.

Powder from animal products like egg or dairy will generally have closer to 25 grams of protein.

If you've never used protein powder, you'll be delighted to know that it's very easy to use.

Here are several ways that protein powder can work for you and your family.

- **Get some protein into your picky kids.** (Or adults, for that matter.) If you have a family member who seems only interested in existing on macaroni and cheese or mashed potatoes, an unflavored protein powder can add a boost of growth-inducing protein to an otherwise nutritionally barren meal.

- **Add it to those low-protein, just-add-water prepper meals**. If you are a person who generally consumes a significant amount of protein, eating those meals is going to sap your normal energy. A couple of scoops of unflavored protein powder (you don't want chocolate in your enchilada rice dish) stirred in at the end can increase your protein intake without changing the flavor of the food.

- **Use it for kids with braces.** Every time my daughter gets her braces tightened, she ends up being unable to chew for several days. I make her thick, delicious shakes with frozen fruit and vanilla whey powder to give her an "ice cream-ish" treat that is still highly nutritious. This is also good for people who have had dental work or oral surgery.

- **Stir it into yogurt.** Give your next yogurt parfait a protein bump by stirring in vanilla protein powder. It will make your yogurt thick, creamy, and delicious.

- **It's speedy and healthy**. Rushing out the door? Don't get tempted by the empty calories of the pastry shop in the lobby. Blend up a quick shake loaded with fruit and protein powder to power you through until your next meal.

- **It travels well.** Measure single servings out into the snack-sized ziplock bags and store those inside a double zip bag. Use one of the shaker cups I mentioned above to mix your protein powder with water for immediate gratification and nutrition.

And don't limit yourself to just drinking it. As mentioned above, the unflavored version can be mixed into all sorts of low protein foods. Try a scoop in:

- Pasta dishes
- Creamy soups
- Baked goods (you'll want to use this to replace some of the flour in equal parts)
- Mashed potatoes
- Foods with creamy sauces
- Purees

For best results (aside from the baked goods), stir the powder in after you've finished heating the food, right before serving.

Selecting Meats

The conventional meat industry is at the root of severe health ramifications across the country. When building your pantry, you want to focus on foods that sustain health instead of harming it. Therefore, you need to keep a few things in mind when selecting the protein sources you wish to include in your stockpile.

Livestock animals that provide meat or dairy products are often tainted with growth hormones, antibiotics, and GMO feed. These items pass through the food chain to the consumer.

First of all, as discussed above, GMOs have been known to cause a variety of health issues. If you've made it a priority to avoid GMOs in your own diet, you need to be sure that you don't unintentionally ingest them secondhand in the meat you've chosen.

Secondly, studies hold growth hormones responsible for various reproductive health issues, including opposite sex characteristics in developing children, as well as early-onset puberty, cancer, and infertility.

Finally, and perhaps most importantly, when we are constantly exposed to antibiotics in our food supply, we run the risk of becoming resistant to them. Illnesses that should be easily eradicated become deadly.

An added concern for many is the unsanitary and inhumane conditions under which many factory-farmed animals are raised. Even if you aren't bothered by that ethically, livestock raised under those conditions will be less healthy and therefore less nourishing.

If you can't afford grass-fed organic meat, at the very least look for options that are guaranteed to be hormone and antibiotic free. The USDA does not allow the use of growth hormones in pork, which makes it a slightly better option.

Here's a little primer on those deliberately confusing meat labels:

- *Hormone-free:* This means something with beef, but is nothing but a marketing ploy when you see it on poultry or pork, as the USDA does not allow the use of hormones with those animals. Hormone-free *does not* mean antibiotic-free.
- *Antibiotic-free:* Because of poor and stressful living conditions, factory-farmed animals are very susceptible to illness. Antibiotic-free means they were not prophylactically treated with antibiotics. This does not, however, mean that the animal is hormone-free.
- *Grass-fed*: Grass-fed cows are allowed some access to the outdoors and are not fed grains or corn. This does NOT mean they are organic, because the grass they are grazing on may have been chemically fertilized and sprayed. Unless you have actually seen them roaming around the farm, keep in mind their access to the outdoors may not be the lovely rolling pastures that you have in your mind, but a crowded corral with hundreds of other cows.

- *Free-range:* This label doesn't mean diddly-squat. It means that the animal is allowed a minimum of an hour a day outside. This could mean that they are crammed into an open area with a billion other chickens, still, without room to move, or that their cage is put outside, leaving them still tightly confined. Like the grass-fed cows above, unless you actually see the farm with the gallivanting chickens or pigs, take the label "free-range" with a grain of salt.

Your best options, if you can't afford organic meats, are to go for the hormone- and antibiotic-free options as a supplement to vegetarian protein sources like local eggs, beans, and organic dairy products.

Purchase in Quantity

One of the best ways to lessen the price of good quality meat is to purchase it in quantity. When you purchase a side or quarter of beef

or pork, you can reduce the price per pound dramatically. Also, the butcher will cut it up in the way that you prefer. You can opt for stewing beef over ground beef, for example, with the lesser cuts of meat.

When purchasing meat in quantity, treat it as an investment. Take the time to locate a source that you can trust. Consider small butcher shops or local farms, and find out how the animals were farmed, keeping the above tips in mind.

Making friends with your butcher or farmer could also put you at the front of the line for meats that they'd like to get rid of before they expire. I recently acquired 5 whole chickens at half price from a local farmer because I was able to take them immediately. Other ways to get in the loop on these good deals are through Internet sources like Craigslist and private groups on Facebook or other social media networks.

Consider Alternatives

Another way to get your protein is through alternative sources that are not your average grocery store fare. Keep an open mind and consider some of the following options:

- Goat
- Mutton (older sheep)
- Game (venison, moose, wild turkey, etc.)
- Rabbit (one of the easiest meat animals to raise yourself)
- Duck
- Goose
- Farm fresh eggs

Learn how to preserve meat

Before you stash that side of beef in the deep freeze, consider the vulnerability of the electrical grid. In the event of a storm that takes out the electricity, you could be without power for anywhere from a few hours to a few weeks. Several years ago, parts of Arkansas and

Missouri were without electricity for 5 weeks due to a freak ice storm that did tremendous damage to the local infrastructure. You could sustain massive losses to your food supply if you are reliant on electricity to preserve such a large investment.

Consider the following ways to preserve meat for your pantry. You can find detailed instructions for several of these methods in the food storage section of this book:

- **Dehydration**: Learn how to dehydrate ham, poultry, and ground beef crumbles. Remember, though, that rehydration can use up valuable water supplies.
- **Making Jerky**: You can make jerky in your dehydrator for an instant protein snack that does not require rehydration. Vacuum seal it to prolong the shelf life.
- **Pemmican**: This is a paste made from meat mixed with natural elements such as berries, roots, and herbs and then dried until it is hard and brittle.
- **Curing/Smoking:** These two methods are low-tech ways to preserve meat without the need for refrigeration.
- **Canning:** This is my personal favorite method of preserving meat. You can make soups or stews, or you can simply preserve meat to be used in recipes in the future. Dinner can be ready as quickly as popping open a jar and heating the contents.

Make the Investment

Use the budgetary strategies discussed in the "Shopping" section of the book to save up enough money to make a large investment in meat. Although it's a lot of money initially, you will save substantially from the price of purchasing in small increments each week at the grocery store. You can store the large purchases in your freezer as you gradually preserve it using non-grid-dependent methods.

How Much Protein Do You Need?

An adult requires at least 50 grams of protein per day for good health, and a prepubescent child needs about 15–20 grams per day. Keep in mind that you may be working physically harder if you are relying on your storage foods because of a disaster or off-grid scenario. This will increase your protein needs. Many health and fitness experts recommend 1 gram of protein per pound of lean body mass. For most people, half a gram of protein will be sufficient to meet their needs.

Of course, few people know how many grams of protein are in various foods off the top of their heads. Just to give you an idea of the amount of protein in a "serving," here are a few examples:

- 1 cup of milk has 8 grams of protein
- 3 ounces of meat has about 21 grams of protein
- 1-cup serving of cooked beans has about 16 grams of protein
- An 8-ounce container of yogurt has about 11 grams of protein
- A 2-tablespoon serving of peanut butter contains 8 grams of protein
- 2 eggs contain 12 grams of protein

Based on this, a ballpark estimate is that adults require 3 servings of protein per day, and children require 2 servings of protein per day.

So this works out to:

1095 protein servings per adult per year
730 protein servings per child per year

Most people consume considerably more than 50 grams of protein per day, so the calculation above should be considered a bare minimum.

Fruits and Vegetables

A major challenge when living from your stockpiled foods is getting enough fruits and vegetables. Without produce, your family can be at risk for nutritional deficiency diseases like beriberi, folate deficiency, scurvy, and Vitamin A deficiency. A lack of fruits and vegetables can also compromise the immune system, and when you're relying on your food storage, it will probably be the worst possible time to become ill. A minimum of 5 servings per day is recommended, but during the long winter, how can you meet that goal with the contents of your pantry?

Supplying your family with produce that will provide the necessary nutrients that their bodies need to thrive is a twofold process. Not only should you preserve the summer's bounty for the winter ahead, but you should also come up with ways to add fresh greens outside of the growing season.

Building a Produce Stockpile

When creating your produce stockpile, you have to look at what actually constitutes a "serving" for the people you will be feeding. It may not actually be the amount that you expect. For example, a child's serving of green beans is anywhere between a quarter cup to a half a cup (depending on their age), but an adult's serving is a full cup. So for a small child, plan on 1–3 cups of produce per day and for an adult, plan on 5 cups of produce per day.

Whenever possible, focus on organic produce. Pesticide use in conventional farming has been linked to myriad health problems. The EPA warns of the risk of birth defects, nerve damage, and even cancer after long-term exposure. Especially at risk of harm from pesticides are prepubescent children and fetuses.

Some people may also wish to avoid GMOs (genetically modified organisms). If that's you, particularly avoid anything non-organic that contains corn or soy ingredients.

What to shop for

At the grocery store, look for sales to build your supply of produce:

Dried: Dried fruits such as raisins, banana chips (without sugar), and dried cranberries can pack a lot of nutritional punch into a tiny serving size. Think of them as concentrated vitamins. An adult serving of raisins is only 1/4 cup, which means that you can pack a lot of nutrition into a small amount of space with dried fruits.

Canned: Canned goods such as tomatoes, green beans, and peas can go a long way towards providing nutrition. The benefit to those rows of tin cans is that you don't require power to store them safely, and they are fully cooked so you don't even have to heat them up in a grid-down situation. You can also find many varieties of canned fruit, but beware of heavy syrups, which are often made with GMO corn syrup.

Frozen: Frozen fruits and vegetables are the closest to fresh that you can get. This is a great way to build a stockpile for good times, but don't put all of your produce in the freezer. During an extended power outage, you stand to lose a large portion of your deep freeze contents. If you do purchase a large amount of produce for the freezer, have canning jars, lids, and an off-grid method for canning them if the electricity goes down for the long-term.

Freeze-dried: This is a more expensive option, but freeze-dried fruits and vegetables maintain nutrients, require little storage space, and need no special storage conditions. You can add a great deal of variety to your pantry with a selection of freeze-dried ingredients and the foods, if sealed correctly, can last up to 25 years.

Preserving fruits and veggies

There are many effective ways to preserve fruits and vegetables that you acquire fresh. Whether you harvest them from your own property, buy them at the farmer's market or a local orchard, or even make a bulk purchase from the discount bin at the grocery store, having the supplies and skills to quickly preserve them can allow you to make the most of your windfall.

Dehydrating: Whether you use an actual dehydrating machine, hang the items in a sunny, dry place, or use your oven, dehydrating can be an easy way to store a lot of food in a small amount of space. One drawback to dehydrated food is that you require a substantial amount of water to reconstitute it. Homemade fruit roll-ups are an exception—they are a healthy, dehydrated treat that requires no soaking time and they make a great addition to backpacks and bug-out bags. (A bug-out bag is the bag that preppers have packed and ready to go at a moment's notice in the event of an emergency evacuation or an unexpected hike back home.)

Canning: As always, canning is my favorite way to preserve food. Many fruits can be canned using the water bath canning method, but vegetables (with the exception of tomatoes and pickles) require pressure canning to be safely preserved. I have row after row of sliced fruit, colorful veggies, pickles, salsas, jams, and applesauce lining my shelves and waiting for their turn on the table.

Root Cellaring: Another way to store produce is by root cellaring. Some fruits and vegetables will last the entire winter if they are stored under the proper conditions. Autumn harvests tend to do particularly well when root cellared: apples, garlic, hard squash, potatoes, and carrots can all last for many months.

Fresh Greens: Anytime, Anywhere

If your family is anything like mine, fruits and vegetables make up a huge part of your diet. When we did a one-month pantry challenge, the first thing that we realized was how much we missed fresh produce. No matter how big your pantry is, it's important to be able to provide yourself with some fresh nutrients too. In the off-season or in an apartment or other place with no outdoor growing space, learn to adapt and provide your family with some fresh produce.

- Grow herbs and lettuce in a bright window.
- Set up a hydroponics system in a spare room.
- Go even further and look into aquaponics.
- Create a little greenhouse with a grow light for year-round veggies.
- Sprout seeds and legumes for a healthy addition of greens to salads or sandwiches.

Sprouting

The easiest garden you'll ever grow may be right on your kitchen counter. Anyone can sprout seeds, whether they live on a secluded homestead or in a high-rise apartment.

The greatest thing about sprouts is how much food you can get from a small amount of storage supplies. For example, one pound of beans can turn into 300 or more servings if you sprout them.

You don't have to nurture your sprout garden throughout the summer to get your harvest, either. In most cases, your sprouts will be ready to eat in less than a week.

Sprouts are incredible sources of nutrients, far above the level of nutrients in the actual seed they are started from. At no other time in a plant's life cycle is there as high a concentration of vitamins, and this makes them the perfect food for a long-term disaster.

Different sprouts contain different nutrients, of course. Among them are Vitamins A, B, C, E, and K, and minerals like calcium, magnesium, potassium, iron, zinc, and niacin.

What to sprout:

The sky is the limit with sprouts. Seeds, nuts, beans, and grains can all be sprouted in the right conditions with the proper starter.

Seeds and grains must be kept dormant. It is best to store them in a cool, dark, dry place. Introducing moisture in the storage conditions could cause your starters to sprout too soon, and then die.

The shelf life of starters:

- Nuts: 1–3 years
- Seeds: 5+ years
- Grains: 3–5 years
- Beans: 3–5 years

The supplies you need for sprouting:

Probably the very most common sprout container is a mason jar with a screen over the top. However, this isn't the simplest method.

There are inexpensive trays that are specially made for sprouting darned near anything successfully. (My very favorite one comes from the website Sproutpeople.org and is called The Sproutmaster.)

My setup is a stack of trays that measure 5x6 inches. You can stack as many of them as you want to.

The tray's bottom is made of small holes for drainage. The process couldn't be simpler.

- **Rinse your seeds**. Remove any little bits and pieces that aren't seeds, like stems, twigs, pebbles, etc. (Think about rinsing beans before you soak them and pulling out the yucky bits—this is the same thing!) Use a mesh sieve and rinse the seeds until the water runs clear.

- **Soak your seeds.** Generally, 1 part seeds to 3 parts water is a good ratio. Each type of seed has different soaking time requirements, so you'll have to look this up based on what type of seeds you are sprouting. If you are getting this information online, it's a good idea to write down your times and any special instructions on your seed container. Most seeds soak for 8–12 hours.

- **Skim off floaters.** If you have any seeds floating on top of the water, give them a gentle push to see if they sink down with their buddies. If they float back up to the top, skim them off and discard them.

- **Rinse your seeds.** Sprouting isn't extremely high maintenance because the "crop" is small. However, 2–3 times per day, you have to rinse your seeds. This only takes a few minutes. Use cool water—not cold, just cool. Sproutpeople.org recommends using high water pressure to oxygenate your seeds. I like the sprayer on my kitchen sink for this purpose. In very hot weather, use the coldest water that comes from your taps.

- **Drain your seeds.** It's vitally important to drain your seeds well each time you rinse. Excess water will cause mold or mildew. I usually shake the seeds in their tray to remove as much water as I can.

- **Let them sprout.** For the next 3 days, continue rinsing and draining your seeds 2–3 times per day. Be sure to put them in a place with good circulation. Seeds need to breathe too. If you can safely put them outside, they'll get great circulation there. Mine live on the kitchen counter with the ceiling fan on. Don't close them up in a cupboard if you want an abundant crop of seeds.

- **Photosynthesize your seeds**. After 3 days of rinsing and draining, now it's time for the fun part: watching them become green! If you haven't been exposing them to light, now is the time. Don't put them in hot, direct sunlight. They only need a bit of indirect light. It doesn't take much light at all for them to green right up. I've read that even fluorescent lighting will do the trick, but I always use sunshine.

- **Continue rinsing and draining**. You'll continue the rinsing and draining process described above for 2–3 more days, at which point most of your sprouts will have sweet little green leaves.

- **Remove the hulls**. On the last day before harvesting your sprouts, you need to remove the seed hulls. The hull is the hard exterior of the seed that split open when the seed began to germinate. To remove them, put your mass of sprouts into a big bowl of cool water and loosen them up with your fingers. The hulls will rise to the top and can be discarded or put on the compost pile. Swoosh your sprouts around in the bowl to get all of the hulls out.

- **Do one more rinse and drain cycle.** Let your hull-less sprouts go through one more cycle before you harvest them.

- **Harvest and eat sprouts**. Rinse the sprouts one last time and drain them very thoroughly before putting them in the refrigerator. Put them in a closed container and eat them within 3–5 days.

How do you eat sprouts?

Sprouted seeds are great eaten raw, and this is what most people think of when they envision adding sprouts to a meal. You can top salads, sandwiches, and wraps with sprouts for a big bump in nutrition.

Bean sprouts are a bit denser and are delicious when added to a stir-fry for the last minute or so of cooking. Or, you can turn off the heat and put on a lid and allow them to steam for 2–3 minutes. Don't overcook them or you'll have a gummy, slimy mess.

Sprouted grains can be steamed lightly, then topped with milk, fruit, and maple syrup for a super-nutritious hot breakfast.

How many servings of fruits and veggies do you need?

For truly optimum health, adults should shoot for 5–8 servings of fruits and vegetables per day, and children should get 3–5 servings.

To keep deficiency diseases at bay, the bare minimum for good health is 3 servings per day for both children and adults.

When we did a one-month stockpile challenge, the thing that we noticed most prevalently was that our stockpile at the time was lacking in the area of produce—we always tend to eat fruits and vegetables at the higher end of the recommendations. Now, a huge part of our stockpile is dedicated to produce and part of our plan includes growing produce year-round.

Keep in mind, a serving is approximately half cup of a fruit or vegetable for children and a full cup for adults.

For stockpile purposes, aim for the lower end, and plan to supplement this with a windowsill garden or one of the other recommended methods for adding fresh greens.

1460 servings per adult per year
1095 servings per child per year

Scratch Cooking Ingredients

To be efficient, every pantry requires certain basics that allow for scratch cooking. A good pantry should have everything you need to whip together a pie, a casserole, a loaf of bread, or a batch of biscuits with no trip to the store required.

Many of these basics can be purchased in large quantities. One of my favorite destinations for pantry basics is Amazon, where I purchase yeast, aluminum-free baking soda, and other building blocks of a scratch pantry. I have also acquired 50-pound bags of organic sugar at Bulk Barn for a reduced price. Check into food co-ops like Azure Standard, if it's available in your area, for other great buys. You can also find some great bulk purchases on Amazon by searching for the product you want, then setting the filter for the largest quantity available.

What basics do you need?

To build your stockpile, look through your cupboards and see what you use the most. Every kitchen will be different but below are my most-used items. These are the things that I search out and buy in bulk.

Baking Items:
- Baking soda
- Baking powder

- Yeast
- Powdered eggs or egg substitute
- Cocoa
- Nonfat dry milk

Fats:
- Olive oil
- Coconut oil
- Shortening
- Lard
- Butter

Sweeteners:
- White sugar
- Turbinado sugar
- Muscovado sugar/brown sugar
- Honey
- Molasses
- Maple syrup
- Confectioner's sugar

Other:
- Salt
- White vinegar
- Apple cider vinegar
- Balsamic vinegar
- Black pepper
- Herbs and spices
- Cornstarch (Avoid GMOs: choose organic for corn products)

The Three Types of Pantries

Now you know all about the components of the perfect pantry, but you still don't have a strategy to create your own. There are a lot of different philosophies out there, but I think it boils down to three basic types of food supplies:

- The Bunker Pantry
- The Agrarian Pantry
- The Bargain-Hunter's Pantry

This doesn't mean you are stuck with just one strategy, however. All the types have positives and negatives. Learn about these food storage ideologies and then take the most applicable components for your situation. Combine them to create your own version of the Perfect Pantry. Use strategies from each type to create a stockpile that meets your family's needs.

The Bunker Pantry

This is the most "hardcore" of the food storage types. A Bunker Pantry is the type of food supply that could keep you going for the next ten years without a single trip to the store. Sure, it might be a little bit boring and lacking in variety, but it is a supply that will see you through any disaster while allowing you to remain in your shelter. This type of pantry focuses on huge quantities of long-term foods, repackaged carefully to resist spoilage due to pests or the elements.

If this is the type of pantry you'd like to build, focus on staples such as wheat, rice, dried beans, salt, and sugar. These foods can be purchased in bulk and repackaged by the user, or you can purchase them already packaged up through vendors like the Latter Day Saints (LDS) warehouse or online food storage websites.

Variety can be added to this type of pantry through commercially canned fruits, vegetables, and meats. When looking for sales on these items, be sure to check the expiration dates. If you are storing for the long-term you want to be certain to grab cans with the longest shelf life.

Another great way to add fruits, veggies, meats, and dairy to your Bunker Pantry is through the addition of freeze-dried foods. If properly packaged, these foods can last up to 25 years. As long as you have water to rehydrate these foods, your diet can remain fairly normal throughout a long-term scenario. Imagine how decadent you'd feel, rehydrating the ingredients to make a fluffy cheese omelet with ham and peppers in the midst of an off-grid situation.

It takes a lot of space to store this much food, so generally a dedicated area must be used as a storeroom. Items should be clearly marked with expiration dates, and when that date draws near, the items should be rotated in to the family's kitchen.

The Agrarian Pantry

This type of pantry is the kind our ancestors had. Most of the purchases are made during the growing season and only small shopping trips are needed to supplement this throughout the year.

It combines enough basic staples for the year ahead with enough of your preserved harvest to get you through until the next growing season. (This is primarily the type of pantry that we keep in our family, with a few of the other strategies added to increase the usefulness of our stockpile.)

To build an Agrarian Pantry, stock up on a year's supply of basics like grains, baking items, tea, coffee, and dried beans. Then focus your efforts on acquiring items in season and preserving them when they are at their peak. Try your hand at canning, dehydrating, and root cellaring. Items can be grown on your own property or purchased by the bushel from local farms and orchards.

Look into purchasing a side of beef and a side of pork to add to your pantry. One purchase per year is sufficient for most families, and your price per pound drops dramatically when you buy meat in this type of quantity. Remember not to put all of your faith in the deep freezer, however, because a grid-down scenario could leave you with a smelly mess and a large lost investment. Try canning, smoking, salting, and dehydrating for the bulk of your meat purchases.

This type of pantry must be replenished every year. Basically, the items in your pantry are purchased and put back with the intention of consuming them within the next 12 months. Extra supplies should ideally be stored to make up for shortfalls caused by a poor harvest.

The Bargain-Hunter's Pantry

This is the type of pantry made famous by the extreme couponing shows. Using a variety of strategies, people can amass an enormous quantity of food for very little money. Couponing, sale shopping,

bartering, and buying from outlet stores and warehouses can help to create a pantry full of packaged items.

While this is a great way to get started or to supplement your other strategies, it's my least favorite way to create a stockpile. First, much of what you are acquiring is highly processed. Secondly, without a lot of personal discipline, you aren't building a balanced pantry, but just stockpiling whatever is the cheapest. If you use this method, you must be extremely careful not to end up with a pantry full of carbs, but no protein, fruits, and veggies. (I don't care what the kids say, 25-cent ketchup is *not* a vegetable.)

Warnings aside, you can build up a huge amount of food on a very limited budget and still be relatively healthy if you are a smart shopper.

When building a Bargain-Hunter's Pantry, consider the following suggestions to create more balance:

- Look for the items with the least number of ingredients—don't stock your shelves with chemistry projects, no matter how cheap they are.
- Strive for balance by creating an inventory list to keep in your purse so that you know which types off foods are needed to keep your family healthy. (Are you short of protein sources? Veggies? Healthy fats?)
- Don't add it to your stockpile merely because it's cheap, particularly if your storage space is limited.
- Be sure to rotate the items into your kitchen by expiry date. Often the items that have the deepest discounts are the closest to expiration. You aren't saving money if you end up throwing out spoiled food.

Combine the Best of Each Strategy to Build the Perfect Pantry

The Perfect Pantry combines the three strategies listed above to create the optimal supply for the needs of your particular family.

The key is organization. Keep the following tips in mind to create the best possible pantry.

1. Keep an up-to-date inventory so that you know what you have.
2. Catalog your coupons by type and expiration date.

3. Track the sales cycles.
4. Keep your products rotated into your kitchen so that you don't lose foods to missed expiration dates.
5. Store longer-term foods in optimum conditions to prolong their viability.
6. Maintain a list of what is needed to balance your pantry nutritionally so that you can focus on those items when an unexpected bargain pops up.
7. Buy pantry staples (like beans and grains) in the largest quantities you can manage in order to maximize your savings.

8. Remember the adage "Store what you eat and eat what you store"—it isn't a bargain if you purchase something no one in your family will eat.

9. Supplement your pantry by growing as much as possible in your particular circumstances, even if you are just adding a windowsill herb and salad garden.

10. Tap into your inner hunter-gatherer with strategies like foraging, fishing, snaring, and hunting.

11. Purchase seasonally and in large quantities from local growers (or harvest from your own gardens).

12. Become a food preservation expert and stock up on the necessary tools and supplies.

We'll talk about all of these steps in detail in upcoming chapters.

Prepping for Those with Dietary Restrictions

Another important consideration when building your pantry is the restrictions of family members with food-related issues.

There are many people who must eliminate certain foods or suffer the consequence. Allergies and intolerances are a primary issue for the families of sufferers.

Allergies

Prepping for a family member with food allergies can be as easy as stocking alternatives for the person, or as difficult as having to keep the offending ingredient out of the supply altogether.

In the event of a life-threatening allergy, you may want to completely banish the ingredient from your home. Anaphylactic shock requires quick medical intervention, which might not be available or accessible during a disaster. At the very least, be sure to have up-to-date Epi-Pens, cortisone, and antihistamines on hand.

Dairy Intolerance

Dairy intolerance (also known as lactose-intolerance) is rarely life-threatening, but can make sufferers feel terrible. Many people purchase non-dairy milks from the store, but many of these have a short shelf life.

There are a few products you can stock up on, depending on the type of non-dairy milk you prefer. I always recommend that preppers stock up on items that are the closest to their day-to-day foods as possible, to prevent potential difficulties like an upset stomach or an unpalatable taste.

These are also good options for anyone who follows a vegan or paleo diet.

Coconut Milk: Coconut milk is rich and creamy, making it a favorite for coffee drinkers. The coconut flavor is hardly noticeable. You can purchase it by the case in shelf-stable, 1-liter tetra packs or canned coconut cream. If space is an issue, a company called HealthWorks sells powdered coconut milk in one-pound bags.

Cashew Milk: This is one of the creamier-textured non-dairy milks, making it excellent for coffee. It adds a very slight nutty flavor. So Delicious sells this in 1-liter shelf-stable tetra packs.

Almond Milk: Keep in mind that almond milk can separate when it's heated up. For that reason, some people don't care for it in coffee. You can buy this in tetra packs or make your own.

Oat Milk: Oat milk is one of the best-priced options for shelf-stable milks, and it is high in iron. If you're putting it in your coffee, you have to stir it throughout drinking your cup or it will settle unpleasantly at the bottom. You can find this in 32-ounce boxes.

Rice Milk: Rice milk has a more watery consistency than cashew and coconut milks. It's easy to make yourself or you can purchase it in boxes.

Hemp Milk: Like rice milk, this has a thinner consistency. It is very nutrient-dense, making it a good choice. It is lightly sweetened with brown rice syrup in some brands. Look for a carrageenan-free brand for the healthiest option.

Soy Milk: Many people avoid soy milk due to health concerns, but if you are a fan (it reportedly blends very smoothly with hot beverages) there are some shelf-stable options. It comes in 32-ounce cartons and powder form. Look for organic options only if you want to avoid GMOs. "Natural" on the label is completely meaningless.

Whichever version you choose, remember to watch the expiration dates. These are not long-term products.

Another option is to learn to make your own non-dairy milks from pantry ingredients. If this is your plan, be sure to stock up on supplies like rice or almonds.

Complete directions for making rice milk and almond milk can be found in Section VI (page 169).

Gluten Intolerance and Celiac Disease

There is an almost epidemic hierarchy of wheat-related ailments in America today. At the pinnacle of this is celiac disease. Sufferers are highly sensitive to gluten in any form.

The Celiac Disease Foundation explains:[*]

Celiac disease is an autoimmune disorder that can occur in genetically predisposed people where the ingestion of gluten leads to damage in the small intestine. It is estimated to affect 1 in 100 people worldwide. Two and one-half million Americans are undiagnosed and are at risk for long-term health complications.

When people with celiac disease eat gluten (a protein found in wheat, rye, and barley), their body mounts an immune response that attacks the small intestine. These attacks lead to damage on the villi, small fingerlike projections that line the small intestine, that promote nutrient absorption. When the villi get damaged, nutrients cannot be absorbed properly into the body.

The disorder can cause serious long-term health effects and those with celiac disease should never consume gluten, even in moderation.

---

[*]http://celiac.org/celiac-disease/what-is-celiac-disease/

Not quite as severe, but still highly uncomfortable, is gluten intolerance. People with gluten intolerance can have anywhere from mild to severe reactions to the consumption of gluten. Issues can include digestive upset, bloating, aching joints, skin problems, and a host of other symptoms.

Many of the food storage guides recommend storing hundreds of pounds of wheat and flour, but if your family has a member with adverse reactions to gluten, it's wise to focus your purchasing dollars on grains that are naturally gluten free.

- Rice
- Cornmeal (go organic to avoid GMOs)
- Quinoa
- Oats
- Amaranth

Depending on the level of sensitivity, you may need to purchase these from a gluten-free processing facility.

As far as things like gluten-free pasta and other prepared items go, the specialty products can be pricey. To save money, learn to DIY.

By purchasing grains that are not yet ground, you get several benefits. First, the shelf-life is often longer. Secondly, you can save a fortune from the cost of the specialty flours by grinding them yourself. I have both an electric grinder and an off-grid, manual grinder.

If you are committed to gluten-free eating, you'll recoup your grinder investment fairly quickly. Don't skimp on quality—grinding grains is tough work. The Wonder Mill is a good choice because it comes with a lifetime warranty.

High Blood Pressure, High Cholesterol, and Heart Disease

For those with high blood pressure, high cholesterol, or heart disease, it is important to stock food that is less processed. Many processed foods contain high levels of sodium and saturated fats, both of which can be a cause for concern if you have a family member with these health issues. Sodium can send the blood pressure skyrocketing.

Keep in mind that during a time when you are reliant on your pantry, a prescription that keeps the person's reactions to these foods under control may not be readily available. It's imperative that their diet not exacerbate the issue.

Avoid or limit the following foods when stockpiling for a family member with one of these conditions:

- Hydrogenated oils (these are usually found in highly processed foods)
- High sodium foods (better to add salt as needed)
- Sugar/Carbohydrates (Sugar and refined carbohydrates have been proven to elevate triglyceride levels. This can result in cardiac issues or fatty liver disease.)

Stock up on storage foods in the purest form possible for a family member with any of these conditions. Focus on lean meats, vegetables, fruits, and whole grains.

Diabetes

Who can forget the powerful storyline in the eye-opening book *One Second After* about the girl who was an insulin-dependent diabetic? (If you aren't familiar, it is the prepper classic by William Forstchen that tells the story of a few survivors in a small North Carolina town after an EMP strikes the US.) Particularly in the event of a longer-term emergency, prepping carefully for a family member with diabetes can be a life-or-death matter.

As this book is about food pantries and I'm not a medical professional, I can't advise you about the specific medical concerns for diabetics. I can recommend an excellent series on the topic that is available online from Joe Alton, MD (Dr. Bones). You can find the articles at the following web addresses:

- http://www.doomandbloom.net/diabetes-in-survival-settings-part-1/
- http://www.doomandbloom.net/diabetes-and-survival-part-2-type-1-prevention/
- http://www.doomandbloom.net/diabetes-and-survival-part-3-type-2-prevention/
- http://www.doomandbloom.net/diabetes-and-survival-part-4-treatment/
- http://www.doomandbloom.net/diabetes-and-survival-part-5-natural-remedies/

As far as your pantry is concerned, it's important to understand how a diabetic processes food. Carbohydrates are processed in about the same way as pure sugar, and can wreak havoc on blood sugar levels. This means that a large stockpile of grains will not be usable for the diabetic family member.

The following recommendations are for surviving a crisis and are not necessarily recommendations for everyday life when supplies are easy to acquire.

- The ideal diet for a Type 1 diabetic during a crisis situation in which the availability of insulin is in question would be focused on proteins and fats, with as few carbohydrates as possible. Keep the caloric intake fairly low, and spread the food across 6 small meals throughout the day.
- For a Type 2 diabetic, the ideal diet during a crisis is a bit different. Plan for small frequent meals that are high in fiber, low in fat, and low in carbohydrates. Be sure that the diabetic person remains active.

Both of these suggested diets mean that your stockpile should have additional focus on high-quality protein for the diabetic family member, as well as options that are low in carbohydrates. The grain-filled pantry could be a death sentence for a diabetic family member.

Vegan/Vegetarian

A vegetarian does not eat the flesh of animals, but may consume dairy products or eggs. A vegan does not consume any products that have come from animals, including honey.

If you have a family member who is vegan or vegetarian, be sure to accommodate them with protein sources that do not contain meat, such as beans, grains, legumes, seeds, and nuts.

A variety of plant proteins are needed in order to provide the amino acids necessary for good nutrition. Quinoa, in particular, is an excellent non-meat source of protein and amino acids. The bonus of quinoa is that it stores beautifully, making it a perfect addition to any pantry.

Religious Restrictions

Some faiths have food restrictions, and often those restrictions involve meat. Take into consideration the need for kosher or halal food, as well as restrictions against pork, some game, and certain types of seafood.

Prepping for Babies and Toddlers

Another important consideration in the family pantry is products for infants and toddlers. Many women breastfeed, and this is an excellent choice for providing nutrition and a strong immune system for the baby.

However, even if you breastfeed exclusively, it's important to put back some "just in case" supplies. You're preparing for the potential of a disaster, so although we hate to think about these things, it's not outside the realm of possibility that something could happen to Mommy.

An older child can eat a mushed-up or pureed version of the food you've stored for adults, but they'll still need milk. Young babies won't tolerate reconstituted cow's milk well, the consumption of which could lead to vomiting, diarrhea, and abdominal pain.

You can store shelf-stable organic formula in quantity for times like this. As long as the expiration date doesn't pass, you can donate the unopened formula to a women's shelter or food bank once the youngest child in the group is beyond the age of needing it.

Let me reiterate that mother's milk is the best option. But in the event this is not available, the Weston A. Price Foundation offers a recipe for homemade formula on their website.

---

*http://www.westonaprice.org/health-topics/formula-homemade-baby
-formula/

If this is of interest to you, print off the instructions (due to copyright laws, I can't add the recipe to my book) and add the following supplemental ingredients for this formula to your preparedness supplies:

- lactose
- bifidobacterium infantis
- unflavored high-vitamin or high-vitamin fermented cod liver oil or regular cod liver oil
- high-vitamin butter oil (optional)
- expeller-expressed sunflower oil
- extra-virgin olive oil
- coconut oil
- nutritional yeast flakes
- gelatin
- acerola powder

Prepping for Pets

You should also be prepping for Fido and Fluffy if you are building yourself a stockpile. Pet food can be very expensive and if you are going through a tough time, you want to be sure that you're able to feed your furry (or feathered or scaled) friends.

Dry Kibble

Dried kibble pet food doesn't have the longest shelf life, but here are a few tips to keep it fresh for as long as possible.

1. Check the "best by" date on the back of the bag. Look for the food that is dated furthest in the future.
2. Leave it in the sealed bag that it comes in—it's designed to keep the food dark and dry. Once the bag is opened, the food will oxidize quickly and lose nutrients.
3. Store that bag in another container. I keep kibble in a galvanized trash can. This prevents pests.
4. Rotate it into the current supply, just like you do the food for humans.

Canned Food

Canned food will last quite a bit longer but will be quite a bit more expensive than kibble. That being said, I have a large stockpile of canned food for my cats. Cats, particularly male cats, are healthier if they have a bit of wet food each day. It can prevent kidney problems that can be brought on by a steady diet of kibble. And if you are dipping into your stockpile because of money problems, you certainly don't want to add a vet bill to your financial burden.

Homemade Food Ingredients

I have been making homemade food for my dogs ever since a recall appeared a while back in which several brands of dogfood were flagged because they contained euthanasia drugs. *Euthanasia drugs.*

The thing that I discovered is that making my own dog food was less expensive than buying the high-quality kibble I'd been getting for them before. The downside to stockpiling the ingredients would have to be the space you'd need to store all the jars.

My Homemade Dog Food Recipe

Here's my homemade dog food recipe.

It's adapted from several different recipes based on the things I'm able to acquire inexpensively. I usually throw in some leftovers and table scraps too. Just remember that for dogs to digest vegetables, they need to be cooked.

And also, before feeding anything to dogs, check to make certain that it is safe for them to eat. Some things that humans eat are toxic to dogs.

- 50% Meat
- 5% Organs
- 5% Egg (I grind up the shells for a calcium supplement)
- 25% Veggies (peas, carrots, sweet potato, spinach, etc.)
- 15% Grains (oatmeal, brown rice, quinoa, barley, and pasta)

I use the slow cooker to cook the meat. I add the grains and dehydrated veggies in the last 2 hours. Add the veggies during the last 30 minutes if they're frozen, or just stir them in when it's finished if they're canned.

I supplement with fish oil capsules (they think it's a treat) and a human multivitamin. I have big dogs—70 and 145 pounds—so they can take a human multivitamin. Be sure to check the multivitamin dosage with your vet.

The foods above can be preserved in the following ways:

- **Meat and Organs**—pressure can.
- **Eggs**—I have chickens, but you can buy freeze-dried egg powder.
- **Veggies**—dehydrate bags of frozen veggies and store for later. Rehydrate them by throwing them in with the grains you're cooking.
- **Rice and other grains**—bagged in Mylar and stored in a bucket.

If you want to make homemade food for cats, it's a fair bit more complicated. Search up a vet-approved recipe and stock up on the various supplements your feline friends require.

Part III
PREPPERNOMICS:
A NEW WAY TO SHOP

Learn a New Way to Shop

It's time to learn a whole new way to shop. Thrift is of the utmost importance if you want to be able to afford to build your pantry quickly.

One of the most common reasons that people give for not prepping is the cost involved. People seem to have this mental image of a bedroom or basement dedicated to being filled to the rafters with cans of Chef Boyardee. They imagine someone going out and spending $5000 at a time for a year's worth of food, or perhaps an 18-wheeler backing up into their driveway and unloading the contents with a forklift.

The fact is, a pantry is a work in progress, and a whole new type of personal economy. You can save a fortune on your food budget by shopping carefully and in quantity.

A well-stocked food pantry is an investment: purchasing food at today's prices is a great hedge against tomorrow's increases. The cost of food will only be going up. Consider the drought that has savaged California, the number one producer of fresh fruits and vegetables in the entire country. Farmers there have been forced to cut back on the amount they produce, due to water shortages. Livestock herds have been culled because farmers can't grow enough to feed them. Winters are longer and more severe in other parts of the country, leading to shortened growing seasons and freak storms that destroy newly planted crops. Your pantry is your insurance against drought, pestilence, bad weather, and rising prices.

Take peanut butter, as an example: Quite a few years ago, I purchased a store-brand peanut butter for $1.88 per jar when it was on sale. The following year, that very same brand in the very same sized jar was $5.99 on sale because of a poor peanut harvest. Each jar of peanut butter on the shelves represented a savings of $4.11—there is no other investment that gives you over a 200% return.

Before I even knew what prepping was, I had a well-stocked pantry because I learned the hard way how quickly things can change.

When I was first married and had a newborn baby, I was struggling to put food on the table with our tiny grocery budget. Then, as life often has it, things got even worse when my husband got laid off. We had a few dozen bags of bagels in our freezer, a few jars of peanut butter in the pantry, and high hopes for the garden we had just planted. Our situation was desperate, and the new addition to our family added to our panic.

As we rationed out our bagels with peanut butter over the next few weeks, waiting for unemployment insurance to finally kick in, my husband frantically searched for a job, and I became determined to never be in such a position again.

Since we had no money for entertainment, the library was my saving grace throughout this time. One day, searching for answers among the shelves, I stumbled upon a series of books by Amy Dacyczyn called "*The Tightwad Gazette*." These three volumes gave me a whole new perspective on grocery shopping, and is still the basic shopping philosophy I adhere to today. (By the way, I highly recommend the books—you can get one big compendium containing all 3 titles. It's called The Complete Tightwad Gazette. Some of it may seem outdated since it was written in the late '80s/early '90s, but the philosophy is as sound as ever.)

The TG recommends something called "The Pantry Principle." It's a process that saves both time and money. The idea is to consistently stock up on items at the lowest possible prices, creating a supply of ingredients at rock-bottom cost. This means sometimes you have to say no to preparing a meal just because it sounds good. You have to discipline yourself to adhere to a whole new way of shopping that does not supply just food for the week, but replenishes your pantry, again, at the lowest possible prices.

When building your pantry, remember that Rome wasn't built in a day—and neither is your food storage! Patience is the key.

Create a Price Book

First, start a "price book"—this is a vital tool. Without it, you can't be sure if that sale is really a sale at all. A price book is simply a notebook that you keep with you when shopping where you write down the price that you pay for certain items. You should always update your price book with the lowest price for these items. This is what allows me to see that one year ago I paid $1.88 for peanut butter and now the lowest price I can find is $5.99, like I mentioned in the example above.

In *The Tightwad Gazette*, Amy Dacyczyn wrote:

My price book is a small loose-leaf binder. Each page contains prices for one item, and the pages are in alphabetical order for quick reference. I include my code for the store name, the brand, the size of the item, the price, and the unit price.

I began by writing down prices on sale flyers and from my grocery slips. I made a few trips to compare prices of specific items. It quickly became evident that not every sale was really a sale. But when I did find a good buy, and I could verify it with months of records . . . what power! I could stock up with confidence.

At first you may think this is too much work and the idea of shopping at so many stores will be inconceivable. It will pay off. A good strategy is to shop at different stores each week of the month so that within a 30-day cycle you can hit them all. We have our shopping system down to once a month with only a few short trips to hit unbeatable sales.

[A price book] revolutionized our shopping strategy more than anything else we did. For the first time we had a feeling of control over our food budget.

It might take you a total of five hours to make up a price book for comparison shopping, but after several years of supermarket excursions, you may discover that your hourly "pay" for those five hours was over $1,000.

You'll discover all sorts of trends with this type of record keeping:

- Your local sales cycles
- When certain items tend to be loss leaders
- Which stores are consistently cheaper for specific ingredients
- Whether a highly promoted sale is actually a good deal or not

- Whether a big package of whatsits is a better deal than individually purchased whatsits at a different store

Speaking of size . . . it matters. *wink*

Always Calculate the Unit Price

Be sure to record the size of the package you are purchasing so that you can accurately calculate the unit price. A unit price is vitally important. If you happen to go to one of those giant, members-only warehouse stores like Costco or Sam's Club, you may discover that although a huge package seems like a good deal, it is actually cheaper to purchase the items in smaller quantities elsewhere.

The unit price tells you the cost per ounce, per gallon, per pound, etc., of what you want to buy.

Just divide the cost by the quantity. Here's an easy-peasy example:

$$\$100/25 \text{ pounds} = \$4 \text{ per pound}$$

The goal is to compare the unit prices to find the best deal. Here's an example of this:

- 2 pounds of chocolate at $3.80
- 1.5 pounds of chocolate at $2.70

In this case the unit is 1 pound, and the unit prices are:

- $3.80/2 pounds = $1.90 per pound
- $2.70/1.5 pounds = $1.80 per pound

You know how most businesses try to convince you the bigger package is always the better deal? That's not always the case. In this situation, the second package of chocolate, although a smaller quantity, is actually a better bargain.

Another reason you must compare unit prices as opposed to simply grabbing a package that looks the same is the sneaky maneuver that food manufacturers use of reducing the contents of a package and selling it for the same price as before.

For example, one company used to sell one-pound cans of coffee. As prices went up, it appeared their price was the only one to remain the same. However, reading the label showed that they had reduced the amount of coffee in the can to 14 ounces. This misleading marketing ploy has become even more common as production prices continue to rise.

Shopping Strategically Will Net Huge Savings in the Long Run

Now that you know you can confidently identify a good bargain, let's move on to the next step in your new shopping style: saving pennies that add up to dollars.

When you find a staple at a good price, purchase in as much quantity as you can afford and reasonably use before it expires. This will allow you to begin building your stockpile. After a couple of months of shopping in this manner, you'll discover that you don't actually "grocery shop" any more—you shop to replenish your stockpile.

Items that you stockpile should be foods that you regularly consume. If you normally eat steak and potatoes, for example, but you fill your pantry with beans and rice, when the day comes that you are relying on that pantry you will suffer from "food fatigue" and you will also feel deprived. Start now by adjusting the food that you consume on a regular basis to foods that will be sustainable in a food storage pantry.

Once you have the hang of it, you can apply this same pantry principle to nearly everything that you purchase. Your pantry doesn't have to stop at the kitchen. Use your theory of Preppernomics to keep your household running smoothly on far less money!

- Soap
- Toilet paper
- Shampoo
- Kitty litter
- School supplies
- Garbage bags
- Toothpaste

You get the idea—anything that you normally purchase, if you purchase it at deep discount, will add up to a tremendous savings.

You may be saying, "Wait a minute, Daisy. I don't have time to run all over the place just to save 10 cents here and 25 cents there. This is ridiculous."

It's not as crazy as it sounds. Here's why.

It's a *cumulative* savings.

Think about a cart full of groceries during a weekly shopping trip. You might have 100 items in your cart for the week ahead, right?

So, let's say you save 10 cents on every single item in your cart. (Which, when you're shopping like this, is a very low savings—you'll probably save far more.)

In a cart with 100 items, you've saved $10 in a week.

If you do that every single week over the course of an entire year, you've saved $520.

If you apply this to everything you purchase, can you see how quickly this could add up for you? You can save thousands of dollars per year *and* have a loaded pantry, ready to sustain you through emergencies.

It gets even better when you begin purchasing in bulk quantities instead of grocery store quantities.

Some Price Comparisons

Let's look at some more math, and you'll see why maintaining a pantry beats out weekly grocery shopping every time.

I purchase my beef in bulk from a local farmer through a butcher shop. They raise hormone-free meat, the cattle are grass fed, the animals are treated humanely, and the quality is superior. Because I purchase 1/4 of a cow each year, I'm able to get all of my beef at $3.99 per pound.

Compare this to the grocery store (and we're only talking about price, not the superior quality of the meat purchased farm direct): the best price this week for stewing beef was $4.99 per pound. The best price for ground beef was $2.99 per pound. The best price for roast was $9.99 per pound. When you average all of these together, I pay slightly more for ground beef and far less for everything else. I also have the added benefit of excellent quality meat that is cut and wrapped to order, and I'm avoiding the nasty chemicals and factory farming practices that taint the grocery store meat. The average grocery store price per pound, on sale, is $5.99.

- Pantry method: $3.99 per pound
- Regular shopping method: $5.99 per pound

Now, for another example, let's look at grains.

When I lived in Canada, I bought organic wheat berries. I paid $17.04 for 10 kg (about 22 pounds). The shipping was $21.78, bringing my total to $38.82, delivered to my door—or $1.76 per pound. I couldn't get wheat berries at the local store. I had to drive an hour and 15 minutes to get them, resulting in a tank of gas. At the closest place I could find wheat berries, the cost in bulk is $2.60 per pound. Yes, I could buy a smaller amount, but purchasing the larger amount also results in savings because of fewer trips to the store.

If you think back to the last section, the calculator recommends 300 pounds of wheat per person per year. This would be wheat for making bread, pasta, cookies, and other baked goods. If you are buying your wheat already processed into bread, pasta, and cereal, the price continues to climb.

- Pantry method: $1.76 per pound
- Regular shopping method: $2.60 per pound

At $1.76 per pound, that costs $529 per year. *Per person.* At $2.60 per pound, that costs $780 per year. *Per person.* If you can do this with all of your staples, you will see the savings that can be achieved. That is over $1000 per year for a family of four, for just one item.

Some of the things I buy in extremely large quantities are:

- Beef
- Sugar
- Wheat
- Cornmeal
- Oatmeal
- Coconut Oil
- Quinoa
- Beans
- Popcorn

- Tomatoes (although now I grow the 3 bushels per year I've been purchasing)
- Dry milk

You'll be astonished at how life-changing it is to shop for your pantry instead of to fulfil your weekly grocery list. Stock up and prepare for that rainy day that could be just around the corner. And if the rainy day never comes, you've saved time and money while providing healthy food for your family.

Map Out Your Shopping Trips with the Precision of that Annoyingly Hyper-Organized PTA Mom

We all know that one mom, right? She organizes the bake sale like she's plotting to lay siege on a small, oil-producing country in the Middle East. She's so downright scary that you wouldn't dare try to sneak in store-bought cookies on a plate from home.

If you're driving without a plan all over the place to hit the sales, you aren't really going to save enough money to make it worthwhile in most cases. You should shop with a plan in order to maximize your time and fuel costs.

Most areas distribute free weekly flyers to your house. In some places now, these are delivered via email, and it's well worth subscribing to their list for planning purposes.

These are good for more than just lining the bottom of the litter box. These sales flyers will help you to identify "loss leader" items that are geared to get customers in the doors.

The loss leader is simply the unbeatable, oh-my-gosh-what-a-sale bargain to get you in the door, at which point they hope you'll purchase other dramatically overpriced items just because you're there. This is a technique usually used by big corporations, so I have no qualms whatsoever about beating them at their own game and stopping JUST to purchase the loss leader items in quantity.

It isn't always worthwhile to go far out of your way to purchase the loss-leaders, though. You have to establish a sensible route and pick up sale items along the way. Wasting half a tank of gas just to save 50 cents per item isn't thrifty at all.

- ✓ Spend a couple of hours each week writing down the sales that seem good.
- ✓ Check your price book and compare the unit costs. Are the advertised items really a good deal?

Your List Is Not the Law

A list is merely a guideline. While I do recommend making a list, it's vital to remember, the list is not the gospel. You know how some of those websites preach strict adherence to your lists and menus? Ignore them!

Here's why: Let's say you have a whole chicken on your list, but chicken is outrageously expensive this week. However, pork is on sale. Doesn't it make a lot more sense to take that into consideration and adapt your menu? Be flexible.

For the thriftiest possible shopping trip, your list should include:

- Items that you have coupons for
- Sale items, listed by store, that are a good deal
- Must-have items, like milk if you have small children (there should be *very few* must-have items—flexibility is the key to a bare-bones budget!)
- Ingredients that you require for your meal plans (again, this should be flexible—also, don't waste money on an ingredient that you can only use in one dish if your budget is tight!)
- Map your route before you go—if you have several stops to make, do so efficiently and without backtracking.
- Organize your lists by store

If a store is out of the way from the other shops you plan to hit, think about the week ahead. Do you have any errands or obligations that will take you to that store?

There is a warehouse store about an hour away from us. Any time we have an appointment in that city, we plan ahead to allow some extra time to stop at the warehouse store and stock up.

When embarking on an afternoon of sales shopping, it can be a good idea to put some ice in a cooler for housing perishable food. If possible, plan to pick up most of the perishable items on your last stop.

Here are a few more tips to help you keep the budget under control if you are spending an afternoon stockpile shopping:

- Eat before you go—hunger can impair your judgment because everything just looks so darned good!
- Take a bottle of water or a cup of coffee with you so that you aren't tempted by the coolers or the Starbucks at the front of the store.
- Go alone—it is always far more expensive with a spouse or a child in tow. Admit it, who among us hasn't bought something frivolous just to make another family member shut up happy?

Use the Envelope Method for Budgeting.

Speaking of keeping your budget under control, consider the envelope method for creating your stockpile.

It's really easy to see a great deal, make a large purchase, and then realize you don't have enough money to pay an important bill or to take care of another necessary expense.

When you figure out what you can afford to spend on food, put that money in an envelope earmarked specifically for that. If you have a little left over at the end of the week because there weren't any good bargains, leave it in the envelope and put it towards a large bulk purchase later. Alternately, when you are out of money, stop shopping.

If we all diligently applied the envelope method to our lives, it sure would be a lot harder to be deeply in debt.

It really *is* that simple. When you buy food or other items for your stockpile, pay for these things separately and tuck the receipt into your envelope. This will help you to keep track of your spending.

Build Your Pantry Strategically

Focus on building your pantry strategically. What are your priorities? For us:

- The priority is clean, healthy, organic food.
- I am prepping for 3 people and 4 pets.
- We face frequent power outages because of high winds up in the mountains. This means that frozen food and long cooking times are not practical.
- I'm not rolling in bathtubs full of money, so I want to have plenty of food to see me through the coming inflation of food prices.

With these thoughts in mind, I select food for our household based on local sales, the clearance rack, my garden, and my access to local farms and orchards. I also purchase organic grains in bulk quantities from some online sources.

Answer the following questions to help figure out your priorities and create a plan:

- How many people are in your family?
- How many pets do you have?
- What are the likely scenarios you may face in your current location? (Think about weather conditions, proximity to natural threats, etc.)
- What kind of budget can you allot to prepping?
- Do you have family members with special dietary requirements?

Part IV
CREATING YOUR PANTRY

You Don't Know What You Need Until You Know What You Have

The very first step to building your new prepper's stockpile isn't a shopping trip.

It's an inventory.

There's good news and bad news.

First the good news: In most cases you'll discover that you have a lot more than you think you do.

Now the bad news: You're about to make a heck of a mess.

1. **Pull out every bit of food in the house that doesn't belong in the refrigerator.**

Clear your counters and table and empty out your food storage areas completely. Now, while they're empty, is a perfect time to clean out your storage areas. I like to clean areas that are going to store food with the most natural products possible. You can use vinegar and water, or a nontoxic cleaning product. I'm a big fan of the Method brand or Mrs. Meyer's brand. (Mrs. Meyer's is expensive, but wonderful.) Scrub everything down and then leave it open to air out while you're organizing your stuff.

You won't want to pull all of your freezer items out where they'll thaw. Simply pull them out for long enough that you can write down what's in the freezer and in what amounts.

2. Sort it into categories

Now that you can see everything, it's time to sort it out. Put similar items together. You might categorize something like this:

- Baking supplies
- Pasta
- Rice
- Boxed food like flavored pasta or rice dishes
- Canned meat like tuna or chicken
- Canned fruit
- Canned vegetables
- Crackers
- Cereal
- Jars with sauce (marinara, salsa, cheese)
- Cans of soup, stew, and chili
- Mixes (pancake, brownie, cake)
- Dried fruit
- Treats like cookies, chips, etc. (Items with little nutritional value)
- Granola bars

3. Make a list of what you have

Now that you have everything out, are you surprised by anything? Do you have more or less than you thought you might?

Now it's time to put it all down in black and white. This probably won't be your permanent pantry list, it's just a starting point.

When you write down your quantities, do it in the way that makes the most sense to you. Some people like to use the weight, for example:

6 pounds of pasta

Others, myself included, like to quantify it in realistic serving sizes. By realistic, I mean a size your family members would actually consume at a meal, not the 1-ounce servings touted on the package.

24 servings of pasta

Quantifying by serving size doesn't work with things like baking soda or flour—for those items, weight measurements will be the most accurate.

4. Figure out meals you could make with these items

Now, pretend you have no food except for this. Regardless of what the calculators tell you about how long your supply will last, a meal that consists of raisins, rice, and canned green beans might not be your idea of a meal.

So, using ONLY the items you have on hand, how many meals could you make that your family would want to eat? How many meals are just lacking 1–2 ingredients to make them perfect? Start a list of those missing ingredients.

Are you taking some staples for granted? For example, if you're considering cereal a meal, do you have a source of shelf-stable milk? For baked goods, are you assuming eggs are available? There are shelf-stable substitutes available for this too.

5. Figure out how much you need

Remember back in "The Perfect Pantry" section when we figured out how much food we needed in our pantries? If you didn't do the calculations then, do them now.

6. Make an ideal meal plan

This is going to sound crazy, especially considering the fact that we are preparing for scenarios that are outside of our normal life, but the next thing I want you to do in this preparation stage is to make a meal plan for a normal month.

Include in it your family favorites: maybe it's oatmeal for break-fast, sandwiches for lunch, and a dinner of meatloaf, mashed potatoes, and a vegetable. Maybe you have a tradition of Saturday morning pancakes. Put that in, too. Is there a special meal for celebrations in your family? Even in differing circumstances, birthdays, anniversaries, and achievements will happen and they should be celebrated.

While the primary goal of your pantry is keeping you nutritionally sustained, there's another goal that people often forget about.

Having "normal" food means that you can provide a sense of comfort during an extraordinary time. Children will have meals that are familiar, and less food will go to waste. (Waste is something we'll discuss in upcoming chapters. When you are reliant on your pantry, the waste of food is a sin that could be deadly.) When everything in your life is in turmoil, the comfort provided by a favorite food or beloved tradition can't be overrated.

Now you know what you have . . .

- Are you surprised?
- In a good way or a bad way?
- Do you have as many supplies as you thought you did?
- Do you have *more* supplies than you thought you did?

Analyze this list like it's the key to a map that leads to the Holy Grail. This is your starting point. In a few months, you'll compare your supplies then to this list and feel a major sense of accomplishment.

Finally, It's Time to Go Shopping

You've been plotting the creation of your stockpile. You've taken inventory of what you already have. You've made a meal plan. You know why you need to build a pantry, and since the timing is getting more imperative by the day, now you just need to start doing it.

There are two ways to get started, and which you choose depends on the status of your inventory. You might be starting with a completely empty pantry, or you may have some basic supplies on hand.

Either way, you need to focus first on building your supply so that you have everything you need to begin cooking from scratch as soon as possible. Below, we'll talk about the two different starting points. The pantry-building plan will only be different during the first few weeks.

Pantry A: Getting started when you have some supplies:
Most people will fall into this category.

It's a lot easier to get started if you've got a few things in your cupboard. If you already have spices, condiments, and a few meals worth of food, you can free up some of your grocery money for stockpile purchases.

If that's the case, double up on some of the items on List #1.

Pantry B: Getting started when your cupboards are bare:
Some folks will start with nothing.

While that may seem hard to wrap your head around, there are many valid reasons that might be the case:

- Maybe you just undertook a long-distance move.
- Maybe your home was destroyed by fire or flood.
- Maybe you live in a city and have been, up until this point, a daily purchaser of take-out food.
- Maybe you've been living with others and just moved out on your own.
- Maybe things have been rough, and you've been living hand-to-mouth and you are looking for a strategy to make life a little easier.

When making your first shopping list, you must consider foods that can pull double duty as "right-now" meals and as "storage food." When you have absolutely nothing on hand, the challenge is keeping your family fed while you put aside money to make bulk purchases.

When you are starting with bare cupboards, you can break down your shopping into two types:

1. Shopping for weekly groceries
2. Shopping for the stockpile

The weekly groceries are the fresh items that you get for the meals you are making throughout the week—I call this "right-now food." Items like meat, dairy products, eggs, and produce make up the bulk of it. The stockpile groceries are the larger purchases of items that you are putting away in the pantry for later use, as well as the staples that you need to cook from scratch—this is your "later" food.

If you're starting with nothing, you may need to pick up some shortcut foods you wouldn't normally eat. For example, that first week, you might need to grab some canned soup and bread for quick, thrifty lunches, whereas later, the majority of your food will be wholesome, delicious, made-from-scratch items.

Be sure, however, not to focus ONLY on "right now" food. It's imperative to pick up a few pantry basics each week. Your meal plan will be simple fare, but that's okay, because you have a goal to meet!

Meal Planning While Starting Your Pantry

It's really easy to get sucked into purchasing food for the here and now, and to forget about creating a stockpile. We live in a "just in time" society, where people in metropolitan locations often grocery shop that very day for the evening meal. Many people are completely reliant on the delivery of foods to the grocery store, and if that delivery is interrupted, they'll be up a very unpleasant creek without a paddle in sight.

And here is one very simple fact: *It's hard to cook from scratch with an empty pantry.*

I'm a big proponent of cooking from scratch. It tastes better, it's more frugal, and it's far healthier. You know exactly what is in a loaf of bread that you make yourself from simple ingredients, but a loaf of bread in a cellophane package often bears a list that reads more like the supplies for a chemistry project than a compilation of ingredients.

I know, I know. My website is called "The Organic Prepper" so you probably never thought you'd see me recommending packaged food of any type. But, in a bare cupboards situation, it is a little bit tricky, particularly in the first week or two, to make everything completely from scratch. And if you're broke, it's even harder to get started. Fam, I've been there.

Remember how I said that I started this project with absolutely nothing in my kitchen? When I say I was starting with completely bare cupboards, I mean COMPLETELY BARE. Not so much as a packet of ketchup was thrown in a drawer. I did not have a single spice, not even salt or pepper. Nor did I have any pantry basics yet, like white vinegar, baking soda, yeast, condiments, or sugar. If I were to go and stock my cupboards totally with those items, it would take the entire week's budget, and I wouldn't be able to afford the right-now foods: ingredients like fruits, vegetables, meat, eggs, and dairy products.

Here's an example: if you wanted to make a loaf of bread and a pot of beef and vegetable soup, you'd have to purchase all of the ingredients separately.

Think about the list of ingredients required for this:

- Flour
- Salt
- Sugar
- Yeast
- Milk
- Oil
- Broth
- Ground beef
- Barley
- Assorted vegetables
- Tomato paste
- Garlic
- Onion
- Spices
- Salt and pepper
- and to make it a little nicer, butter and Parmesan cheese

Within a month, you'll have enough basics to make this practical, but initially, that meal would be a large percentage of your budget for the week. So, in light of that, you may have to take some short-cuts. To start out, plan a few inexpensive off-the-shelf meals to make it possible to put aside the money for those pantry basic purchases.

I can't express strongly enough how important it is *not* to be married to your menu. I know we've discussed this before, but I just want to reiterate it: if you go to the store and chicken is outrageously expensive but ground beef or pork tenderloin are on sale, then roll with it.

Always be ready to modify your menu and base it around the items you can get at a good price. Meat and produce are the items that have the most fluctuation, so always be flexible and prepared to improvise.

This is Prepping 101 and the ability to adapt is valuable in many different situations.

Shopping List #1

First, let me introduce the shopping lists. These lists are not engraved in stone. These lists are a basic guideline to get you started. You need to figure in these variables and adjust the lists as needed:

- Your budget
- The preferences of your family
- Your level of cooking skills
- The sales in your area
- The time of year (buying things in-season is a huge money saver)
- The number of people you're feeding

The first week's shopping trip should net you about a two-week supply of food, or perhaps a bit more if carefully rationed.

I have not included quantities for most of these items because you'll need to decide on that based on the variables above.

Look for good buys on couscous, oats, rice, and pasta for grains.

When purchasing fresh fruits and vegetables, look for large quantities. Bagged apples and oranges are generally less expensive than individually selected ones. Large bags of whole carrots, potatoes, and onions are usually reasonably priced. Choose other produce only if it is in season and a good price.

The first shopping trip is always the trickiest—especially if you're a Pantry B family and you have to purchase things like condiments, spices, and pantry basics.

This list includes those types of basics. If you are a Pantry A family, simply omit the things you already have and double up on "later" food like dried beans, rice, and canned tomatoes. And just because it's on MY list, don't get stuff your family won't eat. This is a guideline.

- Milk
- 1 pound of butter
- Square of Parmesan
- Cottage cheese
- Greek yogurt
- Bread
- Eggs
- Peanut butter
- Dried beans
- Whole chicken
- Roast (beef or pork)
- Ground beef (try to get at least one extra package for the freezer)
- Small ham (half for sandwiches or breakfast, and half for recipes)
- Breakfast cereal
- Rice
- Dry pasta
- Canned soup
- Canned fruits and vegetables
- Cans of crushed tomatoes
- Frozen fruits and vegetables
- Fresh fruits and vegetables
- Potatoes
- Popping corn
- Garlic
- Onions
- Olive oil
- Ketchup
- Mustard
- Coffee
- Tea
- Jar of jam
- Basic spices: garlic powder, onion powder, oregano, seasoning salt (MSG-free), sea salt, black pepper, paprika
- Sugar
- Baking soda
- Baking powder
- Flour
- 10 gallons of spring water (5 to drink and 5 to put back)

From here on out, things will be easier. Now you have quite a few pantry basics that will make scratch cooking easier, like baking soda, baking powder, flour, and spices. These "support items" will last much longer than a week.

Menu #1

This might be very different from the food you've been eating, so here's a sample menu using the above items. *(A * indicates that the recipe is in the final section of the book.)*

Breakfasts
- Ham, eggs, and toast
- Cereal with milk
- Yogurt with fruit
- Pancakes with butter and warmed jam topping

Lunches
- Peanut butter and jam sandwich

- Can of soup
- Baked potato with butter and Greek yogurt
- Leftovers from the previous night
- Ham sandwich
- Fruit salad with yogurt

Dinners
- Pot roast with potatoes and carrots*
- Stew made from leftover pot roast and vegetables* (serve over rice or noodles if you need to extend it)
- Spaghetti made with crushed tomatoes, ground beef, and herbs, topped with Parmesan*
- Spaghetti pie*
- Slow cooker ham and potatoes*
- Potato soup*

Snacks:
- Fruit
- Veggies
- Peanut butter sandwiches
- Popcorn
- Yogurt

As you can see, we're stretching the leftovers as far as possible by creating an entirely new meal with them. Breakfasts and lunches are very simple, but filling, with a family dinner being the highlight of the day.

It can be helpful to dedicate one shelf of the refrigerator to foods that are off-limits for snacking. There is little more frustrating than going to make a meal and discovering that a hungry family member ate half of your ingredients.

Lest your kids stage a rebellion, have another shelf of the fridge that has food to which they can help themselves. It's really essential that the entire family sticks to the menu to allow you to control costs at this time.

Beverages and Your Budget

Did you ever stop to consider how much of your grocery allotment is dedicated to beverages?

If your kids drink soda pop, juice, and milk throughout the day, you are most likely spending a fortune on drinks. It's time to switch to water for between-meal refreshments. If they absolutely refuse to drink water, you can make iced tea for an inexpensive refreshment.

In our home, coffee, tea, and water are free-for-all drinks. Everything else is served only with meals. We have a certain amount of juice and milk to be used as beverages through the week, and when it's gone, it's gone. Soft drinks are purchased only for parties. A glass of fruit juice is allotted for breakfast, and a glass of milk for dinner.

When I first switched to this method of refreshment, my family nearly united to take over the refrigerator in a coup.

I'm happy to report that now, after a period of adjustment, the kids voluntarily reach for a glass of water throughout the day and get the majority of their nutrients from food instead of drinks.

Shopping List #2

When meal planning during the building phase, your meals should either be simple and inexpensive, or they should contribute to the creation of the stockpile.

Sometimes the meal you cook today can actually help you in building your stockpile.

Take a whole chicken, for example.

If whole chickens are on sale, it can be an amazing investment for your stockpile. You can get a lot of mileage out of a chicken if you practice some black-belt frugality. Turkeys are even better, and when they go on sale after the holidays, I buy at least two if I can afford it.

First, enjoy a roasted chicken. Throw in some inexpensive veggies like potatoes and carrots, or cook a big pot of rice or couscous to go on the side. This is a nice Sunday dinner that, depending on the size of your family, may leave you some leftovers for one more meal.

Second, try a meal that is light on the meat for using up the rest of the poultry. I generally make a casserole, stir fry, or pasta dish to use the rest of the "better" leftover chicken.

Then, make broth. Simply pop the carcass into the slow cooker with a head of garlic and a couple of onions. Cover it with water and simmer it overnight (8–12 hours). You can add some herbs to the pot also—but if you are going to can the broth, do not add sage. (I learned this the hard way—when canned, the flavor of sage turns very bitter.) You can freeze the broth or can it to begin building your home-preserved stockpile. *You absolutely, positively MUST have a pressure canner to safely preserve your homemade broth in jars—no exceptions!* See the next section of this book for basic canning and freezing instructions.

Other meals that will add to your stockpile are homemade soups or chilies. They will provide you with "right now" food and "later" food—and both will be a wonderful home-cooked meal. Make a great big pot of whatever soup you fancy, leave some out to eat right now, and pressure-can the rest.

Look through your favorite recipes

Take a look at your family's favorite recipes and search for the ones with the least number of ingredients. This is another good way to cook from scratch while building your stockpile.

Some recipes with few ingredients are potato soup, a pot of beans and rice, tomato soup, or a slow cooker roast with potatoes and carrots. Think simple when you are building your stockpile and save the fancy stuff for later when you are well-supplied. Keep in mind that if you have to constantly run to the store for extra ingredients, you are defeating your purpose. You're spending extra money on gas, you are spending valuable time, and it's hard to keep your budget under control when you are constantly adding $5 here and $10 there.

Base the next list on your simple menu plan

So, during week 2, we're going to begin to build out our stockpile a little bit. You will have some basic supplies left over from week 1, and this week, you'll add to that with the following guideline:

- Milk (2x the normal amount)
- Cheddar cheese
- Eggs
- Bread
- Whole chicken
- Ground beef (Try to get at least one extra package for the freezer)
- Small ham (half for sandwiches or breakfast, and half for recipes)
- Quick-cooking oatmeal
- Frozen fruits and vegetables
- Fresh fruits and vegetables
- 1 gallon of white vinegar
- Baking cocoa
- Coconut oil
- More spices: chili powder, basil, thyme, parsley, ginger
- Soy sauce
- Brown sugar
- Yeast

And the following duplicates of the previous week for the stockpile:

- Peanut butter
- Dried beans
- Rice
- Dry pasta (including macaroni)
- Canned fruits and vegetables
- Cans of crushed tomatoes
- Coffee
- Tea
- Flour
- 10 gallons of spring water (5 to drink and 5 to put back)

This week, we have added some more scratch basics, plus some extra goodies for our stockpile. You might notice that the list doubles the milk purchase but doesn't add more dairy products. That's because now, you're going to learn to make your own yogurt and cottage cheese. (Find directions in the recipe section.) If frugality is high on your list of priorities, you'll love how much money you save, particularly if you opt for organic dairy products.

Menu #2

Breakfasts
- Ham, eggs, and toast
- Cereal with milk
- Yogurt with fruit
- Pancakes with butter and warmed jam topping
- Oatmeal with brown sugar and fruit

Lunches
- Peanut butter and jam sandwich
- Can of soup
- Baked potato with butter, cheese, and Greek yogurt
- Leftovers from the previous night
- Ham sandwich
- Fruit salad with yogurt

Dinners
- Roasted chicken with potatoes and carrots*
- Chicken fried rice*
- Chili*
- Chili mac*
- Leftover buffet

Snacks:
- Fruit
- Veggies
- Peanut butter sandwiches
- Popcorn
- Yogurt
- Haystack cookies*

Finally, some variety! You may have noticed the last dinner entry for the week, "leftover buffet." This was a Thursday night tradition in my family when the kids were younger. On Thursday, I pulled out all of the leftovers for the week and put them out, buffet-style, on the counter. The girls could then pick and choose their meal from the odds and ends that weren't quite enough to feed everyone. It was the easiest way to get rid of the leftovers, and everyone was happy. Added bonus: no-cook night for Mom!

Shopping List #3

This week is going to be a little different. We're going to assume there's a bit of ham leftover from last week, since no recipes on the menu called for it. Our list for "right-now food" will be much shorter this week, and the focus will be on pantry basics and the stockpile.

For the stockpile purchases, this is the week to start really investing in those loss-leader purchases. Since that will vary, based on where you are and the time of year, much of this week's list will be up to you. Also, remember how we purchased bread before? This week, we'll add some quick-cooking breads to our menu.

- Milk (2x the normal amount)
- Eggs
- Butter (get extra for baking)
- Fresh fruits and vegetables
- More spices: cinnamon, nutmeg, allspice, clove
- Organic cornmeal
- Potatoes and onions if needed

And hit the sales! You have enough in your pantry that you can skip regular grocery buying this week and put the additional savings into your stockpile.

Menu #3
This menu is based on stockpile supplies. It's not fancy, but it is hearty. Play around with this based on what you have on hand.

Breakfasts
- Eggs and toast
- Yogurt with fruit
- Pancakes with butter and warmed jam topping
- Oatmeal with brown sugar and fruit
- Biscuits with butter and jam

Lunches
- Peanut butter and jam sandwich
- Can of soup
- Baked potato with butter, cheese, and Greek yogurt
- Leftovers from the previous night
- Fruit salad with yogurt

Dinners
- Pork and beans* with cornbread*
- Mexican beans and rice*

- Chicken and dumplings* (made with your canned or frozen broth and chicken)
- Meatloaf, mashed potatoes, and veggies
- Shepherd's pie*
- Leftover buffet

Snacks:
- Fruit
- Veggies
- Popcorn
- Yogurt
- Haystack cookies*

In the meal plan above, you're utilizing pantry stockpile items, cooking from scratch, and eating some alternative proteins this week.

Shopping List #4

This is the last specific shopping list. This week, your mission is to buy duplicates of the pantry staples that you've been purchasing, plus some right-now food. You should never have only one of anything in your pantry. Always have one in reserve, and restock when you put that last one into play in your kitchen.

- Peanut butter
- Dried beans
- Breakfast cereal
- Rice
- Dry pasta
- Canned soup
- Canned fruits and vegetables
- Cans of crushed tomatoes
- Popping corn

- Olive oil
- Ketchup
- Mustard
- Coffee
- Tea
- Jar of jam
- Organic cornmeal
- Sugar
- Baking soda
- Baking powder
- Flour

- Quick-cooking oatmeal
- Spices: garlic powder, onion powder, oregano, seasoning salt (MSG-free), sea salt, black pepper, paprika, chili powder, basil, thyme, parsley, ginger, cinnamon, nutmeg, allspice, clove
- 1 gallon of white vinegar
- Baking cocoa
- Coconut oil
- Soy sauce
- Brown sugar
- Yeast

This week, you'll want to focus on a simple menu, perhaps repeating some of the meals you've had over the past few weeks. Continue to make your homemade dairy products and baked goods. Be sure to eat or preserve leftovers, and allow nothing to go to waste. At this point, there's no need for special menus. Just take what you've learned to shop and plan meals efficiently.

Subsequent weeks

As we discussed previously, weekly grocery shopping is not the way to quickly build a one-year food supply. Now that you have built a base, you'll be able to easily skip the weekly trips and save up for larger purchases.

To be able to afford large purchases when you are on a regular, week-to-week budget, you have to figure out a strategy. For me, the best way to save up for bigger purchases is to skip a week of shopping and then add the budgets of the two weeks together in order to make some bulk purchases that I ordinarily couldn't swing alongside a week of regular grocery shopping. Other strategies could include:

- Selling something in order to come up with a lump sum of money
- Using coupons to build a pantry
- Taking a part-time job
- Cancelling something that you make monthly payments on

and putting every dime of that money towards your stockpile (cable, cellphone, etc.)

Now, it's time to do another inventory. You've spent the past weeks creating the beginnings of your stockpile. You have enough supplies that the majority of your shopping can be geared towards replenishing and building up your supplies. Your weekly needs should be minimal at this point.

When you go through your supplies, pay special attention to the categories we discussed in the second section of the book, The Perfect Pantry. You'll probably find that you have lots of one type of supply (for me that is usually grains) and just a few items in one category (for me that is often protein.)

So, now that you have your basic stockpile, from here on out, each week's mission is to top up your weakest category and replenish your pantry with the best sales around. Try a rotation of the following focus areas:

Grains:
Make a bulk purchase and get Mylar liners and food-safe buckets for storing it. You can also buy individual bags of rice, flour, cornmeal, and oatmeal, and put these in proper storage containers.

Proteins:
Either hit a really great sale on meat or purchase in bulk from a butcher shop. It is fine to store the meat in the freezer initially, but you need a back-up plan if you have any concerns about a potential power outage. Consider canning or dehydrating some of your meat.

Fruits and veggies:
You can purchase grocery store canned produce, but there are tastier and more nutritious ways to get your fruits and veggies. Freeze-dried vegetables and fruits are shelf stable and quite tasty when reconstituted. These usually come in sealed #10 cans and can be put directly

in your storage room with no further fuss. If it's the right season, you can break out your canning supplies to preserve some local bounty.

Scratch basics:

One thing many people forget is milk. Look for a source of dry milk for your pantry, preferably organic or rBGH-free at the very least.

Store this carefully because it can pick up flavors and odors from other nearby pantry items. Mark the container with the expiration date. If you need other scratch basics, this is your week for things like vinegar, baking soda, yeast, and chocolate chips!

The Latter Day Saints' Warehouse

One larger purchase that I made while building my pantry was 8 starter kits from a nearby Latter Day Saints warehouse (also called a Home Storage Center) for $31 apiece. If they do not sell the starter kits in your area, look for the food sold in #10 cans with a 20-year shelf life.

You can search for an LDS warehouse in your area on their website, and if there are none locally, you can order their products online.

Now, these products are *not* the rock-bottom, cheapest way to purchase this longer-term storage food. I could have gotten the items for less money by purchasing them in bulk elsewhere and then repackaging it myself. However, if you're starting out without most supplies, these kits allow you to add supplies that are already packed in #10 cans, ready to sit on your shelves for the next 20 years if need be. If you don't have food sealers, Mylar bags, food-safe buckets, and other items for repackaging, this can be a great way to build a base of shelf-stable supplies that are pest- and environment-proof.

Meal Prep to Stay on Track

One thing that has greatly helped me stick to my budget over the years is meal prep. When I worked outside the home, Sunday afternoon was always dedicated to weekly food prep. It was absolutely necessary to be able to juggle all of my responsibilities during the week ahead.

Now that I work from home, I usually break food prep into two sessions, but the basic premise is the same.

There are also time-saving benefits to this.

- You only have one big kitchen clean-up. The rest of the week your dishes only consist of your plates and flatware, and the dishes you used to heat your food.
- You can multitask by having several things in the oven cooking at once—this also saves on your utility bill.
- You can also wash and prep all your produce at the same time, and then just wash your colander and cutting board when you're finished.

Throughout the week meals are strictly grab-and-go. If your food is already prepped, dinner can be on the table in 10–15 minutes every night.

What does a food prep afternoon typically consist of?

There are a few tasks that you'll be doing on meal prep day.

- Menu planning
- Washing and cutting up vegetables
- Washing fruit
- Portioning out snacks for lunch boxes
- Doing the baking
- Preparing some basic items that can be used in different ways throughout the week (chicken, ground beef, grains, salad)

When you prepare your food ahead of time, dinner is on the table faster than you can say "drive-thru." Your budget will thank you because you won't require those impromptu pizza deliveries when you just don't feel like cooking. Your waistline will thank you because you won't grab high-calorie, low-nutrient convenience foods. Your health will thank you because you will be eating nutritious, wholesome foods from scratch that nourish rather than deplete.

I usually spend Sunday afternoons in the kitchen with my daughter. We turn on some good tunes, don some kitschy, crazy aprons, and get cooking.

Here's an example of a meal prep task list and menu for our family.

- Yogurt parfaits
- Meatloaf "muffins"
- Baked eggs
- Veggies for steaming
- Roasted brussels sprouts
- Blueberry corn muffins
- Wheat berry pilaf
- Broccoli slaw with bacon
- Veggie packets for lunchboxes
- Bread

We also grind and sift flour for the week. Because that is a time-consuming task, sometimes we skip using the fresh-ground flour and resort to commercial flour in order to speed along the baking. This way, we'll stick to the healthier options. Lunches and snacks are nearly always cobbled together from leftovers. Breakfast is quite often a smoothie.

Here's an example of the dinners we'd make with the foods prepped above:

- **Sunday**: Meatloaf muffins, roasted brussels sprouts, wheat berry pilaf
- **Monday**: Slow cooker–roasted chicken, rutabaga (a new favorite), and steamed veggies
- **Tuesday**: Meatloaf with gravy on homemade rolls, sautéed mushrooms, broccoli slaw, leftover rutabaga
- **Wednesday**: Beef and veggie stew (home-canned) with homemade bread
- **Thursday**: Leftover chicken stir-fried with prepped veggies and wheat berries

- **Friday**: Homemade pizza topped with chicken and veggies
- **Saturday**: A whatever-is-left free-for-all, fondly known as "Leftover Buffet"

Eating During Power Outages

A prepping book wouldn't be complete without some attention to a shelf-stable power outage menu.

When the power goes out, my kids tend to think it's party time. They like it because it means that we are definitely going to play some games, do some arts and crafts, and eat some food we don't normally indulge in.

Do you have back-up cooking methods for heating food when the electricity goes out? In some homes, it isn't that easy. Perhaps you live in a rented home without a wood heat source or an apartment without a balcony for a barbecue. And, in the summer you don't want to fire up the woodstove, and during a storm you don't want to stand outside in the rain cooking on the barbecue.

During a short-term power outage, it can make life easier in many cases to eat things that don't require much in the way of preparation. It can be a good idea to have some specific preps for this situation that require no cooking.

Try to keep the refrigerator door closed to maintain a cool temperature in there for as long as possible. If you do get items from the refrigerator, plan it out so you can quickly grab all the things and then close the door again.

To make life easier, stock up on disposable goods to use during power outages in the event your water service is also interrupted:

- Styrofoam plates
- Paper towels and napkins
- Plastic cutlery
- Baby wipes
- Disinfecting wipes
- Plastic cups

In our cupboard, most of the following items are the organic version. Here are some ideas for your "Lights Out" stockpile:

- Graham crackers with peanut butter
- Crackers with canned cheese sauce
- Saltines with peanut butter
- Fresh fruit (apples, oranges, bananas)
- Canned juice
- Trail mix
- Dry cereal
- Cereal with milk
- Canned baked beans with ham
- Pretzels
- Nuts
- Pudding cups
- Canned fruit
- Jerky
- Pouches of precooked and seasoned rice
- Cookies
- Granola bars
- Crackers
- Dried fruits: apricot, mango, banana, raisins, cranberries, pineapple
- Stuff for sandwiches: peanut butter and jelly, tuna, leftovers from the fridge, Nutella

If your family is anything like mine, you may need to stash your power outage goodies where they aren't readily noticeable or accessible. My kids would love to be able to munch on things like pretzels and store-bought cookies whenever the whim strikes them.

Check out the recipe section for "power outage" recipes.

Do You Have the Need for Speed? Start Here

Generally I write about healthy food. I write about focusing on whole foods without additives, and I firmly believe that is the very best way to build your food supply. I believe strongly in the value of a pantry that you will use day-to-day to nourish your family.

However, if you do not have a food supply waiting in your pantry, sometimes an event occurs that forces you to focus on creating a food stockpile quickly. We saw this happen during the Ebola scare, which thankfully didn't turn into a pandemic that required families to self-quarantine, but could have.

Consider ordering a kit with a month's supply of meals in it. You can buy them in buckets, which makes them easily portable for loading the car to bug out and endows them with a very long shelf life. These aren't going to be the healthiest or tastiest meals, but they'll stand between you and starvation. The better quality kits (which I strongly recommend) are about $150 per person.

You may look at the prices and say, "Oh, I can't afford this." But you have to remember, this is enough food for an ENTIRE MONTH. At $150, that means you're spending only $3 per day on food. It honestly doesn't get much cheaper than that.

On my website, TheOrganicPrepper.com, if you click "shop," you can find links to a huge variety of emergency foods and supplies. There are even gluten-free kits available. The buckets contain meals like:

- Enchilada beans and rice
- Cheese and broccoli bake

- Classic chili mix
- Creamy potato soup
- Corn chowder soup
- Cheddar broccoli soup
- Powdered milk
- Oatmeal with brown sugar
- Italian pasta marinara
- Rice pilaf
- Pasta alfredo
- Stroganoff

You can also find freeze-dried fruits and vegetables, chicken, beef, and definitely some powdered milk. There are products like pudding and peach cobbler in freeze-dried format, too.

Even more important than the little treats however, would be the addition of a high-quality multivitamin and a gentle laxative. Some people, when dependent solely upon MREs or dehydrated foods, become constipated. (Ask any Army guy you know, he'll confirm that unfortunate truth!)

Why Your Carefully Calculated Prepper Stockpile May Not Be Enough

We all prep for different future scenarios. Some of us worry about losing our jobs. Others live in drought-stricken areas and put extra food back to see them through the next lean time. Some believe war is coming . . . there are almost as many reasons for preparing as there are people actually doing the deed. But the common thread is that many of us are working hard to build a prepper food supply to see us through an emergency.

Maybe you've been storing extra food for quite a while and feel confident that regardless of what the world throws at you, your family won't starve. Your stuff is stored in the best conditions you can provide. It's bagged and tagged, dated and rotated—what could possibly go wrong?

You aren't going to like the answer.

In an all-out epic disaster, what would be a plentiful supply with our usual cushy lifestyles won't go nearly as far to keep us well-fed. The increased energy requirements of your new lifestyle could mean that you need double or even triple the calories you are consuming now. Not only that, even the least nutrition-conscious among us have grown accustomed to instant access and a wide variety of foods that keep us fairly well nourished.

But luckily, there are some clever additions you can make now to help boost calories, nutrition, and variety.

What works now wouldn't work after a massive collapse.

We all need a basic number of calories just to stay alive—this is called your Basal Metabolic Rate. But basing your food storage supply on this is an enormous mistake.

Most folks have purchased and stored based on the reality in which we currently exist. But post-collapse, we'd be living a very different reality.

It's very important to remember that once you think you have a one-year food supply, you should continue to build your pantry. No formula can tell you how much you will need to eat.

Stress increases your need for calories, and epic events are nothing if not stressful.

A post-collapse lifestyle would be much more labor-intensive.

- **Moving around on foot or by bicycle uses way more calories than driving a car or taking the train.** A pedestrian reality could be the result of an economic collapse (no money for gasoline) or an event that takes out electronic components in engines, just to name two examples.
- **What if you were responsible for providing your own food supply?** It takes a lot more effort to grow vegetables, preserve them, to raise and butcher livestock, or to hunt than it does to make the trip to the grocery store.

- **Providing your own heat is also calorie-intensive.** Chopping wood increases the energy you need by thousands of calories per week over the current lifestyle of flicking a switch to turn on the central heating. Even if someone else provides the wood, you'll still have to stack it, carry it in the house, and keep the fire going—which still requires more physical work than turning the thermostat dial.

A supply that would last for a year during non-eventful times will probably not stretch that far if you are completely reliant on your pantry. So, while you're probably off to a good start, let's look at some factors that may cause you to revisit your stockpiling plan.

Input needs to match output.

If you are at a healthful body weight, maintaining it boils down to one simple fact—the energy you take in needs to match the energy you expend going about your daily life. A deficit of 500 calories a day will mean you lose one pound of body fat a week—which is great for some of us and not so much for others.

If you currently need 2000 calories a day to keep everything ticking and to maintain your current weight, but your new lifestyle means you will need 3000 calories a day, then by eating the 2000 calories you currently consume you are going to lose two pounds a week . . . every week.

While this might be nice for a while, for many people, it isn't going to be nice on an ongoing basis. Not many people carry enough excess weight to be able to handle a loss like this on an ongoing basis. To put a real-life face on it, during the economic collapse of Venezuela, the average weight loss of Venezuelans has been nearly 20 pounds per year. And if that's the average, it means some of those people lost more than that.

During a crisis situation, maintaining your caloric intake as much as possible can help you to remain healthy.

And then there's a lack of nutrients.

In addition, although you wouldn't starve to death eating a diet of rice and pasta, you would reach a nutritional deficit in a short period of time. This could lead to depletion of vital vitamins and minerals, which in turn will lead to weakness, debility, and deficiency diseases that are rarely seen in the United States.

Don't forget rabbit starvation. If you haven't heard of that, it's a term that was coined by Arctic explorer Vilhjalmur Stefansson, who took part in the ill-fated Greely Exploration in the late 1800s, during which only 6 of the 25 original explorers survived. Stefansson observed that those who ate only rabbit, a very lean meat, ate incessantly but were never satisfied, but those who ate fattier meats like moose, beaver, and fish were satiated. There have been many cases in which "rabbit starvation"—a diet that was absent of fat—was considered the most probable cause of death.

Fats will play an important part in a post-collapse diet. Having just over twice the calorific value of carbohydrates and proteins, fats can add a calorific boost to diets that are deficient in the overall calories consumed.

What extras should you add to your stockpile?

There are things you can add to your stockpile to help stave off the nutritional effects of a collapse for a bit longer. Most of these items will last a very long time if properly stored. These items can help to stave off malnutrition, starvation, and food fatigue in the event of a long-term situation in which our lives dramatically change.

Below are the products we keep in our own stockpile. Feel free to substitute with your own favorite brands or locally sourced items— this will give you a starting point if you are looking for high-quality choices.

- **Vitamin and mineral supplements:** get the best quality ones you can and store them optimally in a cool, dark place.

- **Nutritionally complete meal replacements:** these are useful to have around if someone has been ill and is not yet able to return to a solid diet. While perhaps not the most "whole food" choice, they make a great addition to bug-out bags and backpacks as they have a high calorific value and are protein based. If you get the individual packets as a dry powder to mix with water, they hardly add any weight to a pack.

- **Dry milk:** this adds protein in a shelf-stable format (as well as a sense of normalcy for kids—or grown-ups—who like cereal and chocolate milk.)

- **Additional stored food:** I like a combination of buckets of dehydrated food that take up little space in your stockpile and are already packaged for the long term along with healthy additions like freeze-dried fruits and vegetables. We also keep on hand some vegetable soup mixes, freeze-dried meats, and freeze-dried eggs that can easily be added to other dishes for extra nutrients.

- **Protein powder**: An unflavored version can be added to all of those rice and pasta emergency dishes for a healthy dose of protein. "Gainers" are used by bodybuilders to get a lot of calories in one shot and can be used post-collapse for the same reason.

- **Fats**: I stock coconut oil by the gallon—literally. Not only does it last basically forever, it has about a million different uses. You can get "peanut butter powder" (assuming there are no allergies in the house) to add to shakes or baked goods for more healthy fat. The powder can be reconstituted with water in a 2:1 ratio. Also, if you raise animals for meat, be sure to render the fat for future uses.

Part V
WHAT TO DO WITH ALL THAT FOOD

Protecting Your Food

Let me be blunt.

There is absolutely no point in buying all of that food if you don't intend to store it properly. You can't bring it home and toss it on a shelf in your pantry in the short-term store packaging and expect it to last. And building a pantry is no bargain if you have to throw out food.

You have to protect your food from these enemies:[*]

- **Light:** Sunlight causes photo-degradation of your food, which results in fading and discoloration. Even worse, it breaks down the proteins, fats, and vitamins in your food, resulting in an "off" taste and a reduction in nutrients.
- **Moisture:** Damp basements and cellars are not a good place to store your food. Likewise, if you live in an area with a lot of humidity, this can be a real challenge for food storage.

---

[*]http://readynutrition.com/resources/meet-your-emergency-foods-worst-enemies
_06042011/

Why? Because moisture creates a breeding ground for mold, mildew, and microbes, and consuming the contaminated food will make you very sick. Eventually, the moisture will cause the food to rot, leaving you with a smelly mess. The ideal humidity level is 15% or less.

- **Pests:** Rodents and insects are frequent contributors to the demise of stored food. Many pests are already in the food you bring home from the warehouse. It's a very good idea to freeze grains for 3 days before you repackage it for storage, in order to kill off any larvae that may be residing within. Bugs and rodents are notorious for chewing their ways through packaging made of plastic, cardboard, and foil. Did you know that rats and mice are incontinent? They leak urine wherever they go, and this can cause serious illnesses like Hantavirus.[*]

- **Temperature changes**: Food will store the longest when kept at a temperature between 50 and 80°F. Anything higher or lower will reduce the "lifespan" of the food. In many areas, this rules out places like attics or garages that are not temperature-controlled. Attics in particular can reach temperatures of well over 120 degrees in the summer. If your basement is dry, it can be a good place to store food because the earth around it helps it to maintain the temperature year-round, regardless of the weather outside.

- **Oxygen:** Oxygen can cause food to break down more quickly, causing naturally-occurring oils to become rancid, develop a stale flavor, and discolor. And, bug larvae can hatch and feed in an oxygen-rich environment, contaminating your food. Oxygen, when paired with moisture, greatly promotes the growth of mold.

The good thing is, you can arm yourself with all of the weapons you need to battle these enemies. You can choose safe places to stash

---

*http://undergroundmedic.com/?p=6178

your stockpile. Read on to learn all about how to protect and preserve. (Ha-ha . . . get it?)

Food Storage Tools for Dry Goods

You can briefly store your food in the packaging that it came from
the store in, but honestly, that packaging is *not* created for the long-
term in most cases. Keep the following tools and supplies on hand
for repackaging food to withstand the enemies discussed previously.
You don't have to have every single item listed, but you should have
at least one system in place.

- **5-gallon buckets with gamma lids:** Gamma lids are *so*
  much easier to open than the regular lids; trust me on this
  one. If you opt for the regular lids (they're far cheaper) be
  sure to get a lid opener. These can be quite difficult to open
  and close properly, and a good seal is vital to your food's
  longevity. A good quality bucket can easily be stacked. Try
  to use the same type of buckets for economy of space. You
  can sometimes get buckets for free or just a couple of dollars from your grocery store deli or bakery. (They get them
  almost every day and often throw them out.)
- **Mylar bags**: These bags are used in conjunction with other
  methods to add another layer of protection to your food. I
  like to use smaller bags so that I can just reach in and grab
  one bag to rotate into my current food supply without having to go through the entire oxygen removal and packaging
  process again.
- **Bag sealer**: You can purchase a little gadget specifically
  designed for sealing Mylar bags, or you can go MacGyver
  and use a clothing iron or a hair straightener. (*Personal safety
  note*: Your teenage daughter will get mad if you use her fancy,
  expensive hair straightener in the kitchen to seal bags. You'll
  just have to trust me on this— get a cheap one specifically
  for this purpose.)

- **Oxygen absorbers:** Oxygen absorbers do exactly what they sound like they'd do. They remove the oxygen in packaged foods, which in turn inhibits the hatching of bug eggs and the growth of bacteria. The only downside to an oxygen-free environment is that it can be prime breeding ground for botulism, an extremely serious, potentially deadly form of food poisoning that occurs when moist foods are stored in an environment without oxygen. Speaking of repackaging, keep your oxygen absorbers in a lidded jar until they are needed so you don't reduce their effectiveness.
- **Desiccant packets:** You know those weird little packets in over-the-counter medications and new purses? They're desiccant packets. They moderate the moisture that is present, so they're a must for repackaging food that will be stored in an environment with humidity. They can be used in conjunction with oxygen absorbers, but care must be taken to keep the oxygen absorber and desiccant packet as far apart in the container as possible, as the desiccant can inhibit the ability of the absorber.

- **Vacuum sealer:** A vacuum sealer is very useful if you intend to freeze your food for long-term storage, but you can also get an attachment for your dry goods. A vacuum sealer is a device that helps maintain freshness by removing the oxygen from a package before sealing it. When shopping for a vacuum sealer, look for one that has an attachment to seal jars to add to its versatility. (More on choosing a vacuum sealer in the frozen food section.)
- **Food-grade diatomaceous earth:** Diatomaceous earth is approved by the USDA as an anti-caking agent. It can be used to reduce moisture in foods like grains, legumes, beans, rice, and corn. It has the added benefit of being a natural pesticide, which will protect your food from insects. Only use *food grade* DE. The ratio that is most commonly used is one cup of DE to 40 pounds of grains or legumes.

Trust me when I tell you that YOU WANT TO PACK YOUR FOOD PROPERLY. Shortcuts lead to unfortunate events.

Just ask my kids about the hash brown/weevil incident. Or don't. They may have blocked it out of their mind due to the trauma of their mom accidentally feeding them bugs for breakfast.

Important Dos and Don'ts of Repackaging Dry Goods

DO use oxygen absorbers for foods like flour, white rice, oatmeal, wheat berries, and beans.

DO NOT use oxygen absorbers in things like sugar, brown sugar, salt, and powdered drink mixes. They'll turn into solid bricks.

DO NOT use oxygen absorbers when repackaging things that have some moisture. Moisture + lack of oxygen creates a prime breeding ground for botulism. Do not use oxygen absorbers with foods like barley, brown rice, jerky, dried eggs, nuts, granola, or home dehydrated fruits and vegetables.

DO NOT use desiccants in small bags of food, only in bags that are 2-gallon or larger.

DO use food-grade buckets only. You risk tainting your food with plastic containers that are not food grade.

DO place your food in its original packaging in your deep freezer for 72 hours to kill off any bug larvae and eggs that might be in it.

Step by Step: How to Repackage Food for Long-Term Storage

Did you hit the mother lode of dried beans or other low-moisture food? Let's walk through the repackaging process, step-by-step. I promise, it isn't as complicated as it sounds.

1. Make sure your work surfaces and hands are impeccably clean. There is almost guaranteed to be some spillage, and bargain food is not such a bargain if you have to throw it out.
2. Gather your supplies: buckets, lids, Mylar bags, oxygen absorbers, desiccants, food.
3. Get the tools you need: large measuring cup (mine is 4 cups in size), bag sealer, something to stand your bags in. (I use a large baking dish for standing the bags in.)
4. Stand a Mylar bag in the baking dish.
5. If you are using a desiccant, put it in the bottom of your Mylar bag.
6. Use your measuring cup to transfer food from the original package to your package.
7. Put one oxygen absorber in the food at the halfway point, and put the second absorber on top.

8. Leave about 3 inches of headspace at the top of the bag so you have room to seal it properly.

9. Fold the Mylar bag down several times to remove most of the air.

10. Using your bag sealer, gently run it across the top of your Mylar bag, leaving the last little bit unsealed so you can push out any remaining air.

11. After pushing out the remaining air, complete your seal.

12. Place your Mylar bags into your food-safe bucket. You can put a couple of oxygen absorbers in the top of the bucket before closing it tightly.

It's that easy! Continue this process until all of your food is properly stored away.

How many oxygen absorbers do you need?
- 100–200 cc per quart
- 300–500 cc per gallon
- 1000–1500 cc per 5-gallon bucket

Freezing Food for Storage

This is probably the least ideal method for storing food in the prepper world. Why? Because in the event of a one-week power outage, you could lose everything you have stored there, leaving you with a spoiled, smelly mess.

Because your frozen food is dependent on the delicate power grid, it's essential to have an off-grid method of preserving anything in your freezer. Have canning jars, lids, and any other necessary supplies on hand for this purpose if you plan to use your freezer for food storage.

That being said, I have a freezer that contains some meat, veggies, fruit, and the odd pizza. It's not chock-full, and these are the foods we turn to first, sort of our 3-month supply as opposed to a long-term food supply.

The lifespan of frozen food is anywhere from two months to one year. After that point, it begins to lose flavor and vitamins. Proper packaging can help lengthen the time that your food can be stored in the freezer.

After power outages, the second enemy of your frozen food supply is freezer burn. Freezer burn occurs when air reaches the surface of the food, then freezes on it in little crystals. This causes discoloration and an "off" flavor. Although it is *not* a food safety issue, it can negatively affect the taste and appearance of your frozen goods.

A vacuum sealer is very useful if you intend to freeze your food for longer than a few weeks. It helps prevent freezer burn by removing the oxygen from the package before sealing it.

Some models offer bags that can be washed and reused. Although they are a greater investment initially, if this is a tool you will use frequently, it will save a great deal of money in the long run.

You can use your vacuum sealer to repackage meat from the butcher, leftovers (leaving you with a handy meal in a bag that just needs to be thawed and reheated), fruits, and vegetables. Following are some important tips on food storage in the freezer:

- According to the Foodsaver website,* you should not vacuum-seal mushrooms, garlic, or soft cheeses, due to the risk of botulism.
- Cruciferous vegetables have to be blanched and cooled before vacuum sealing. They emit a gas that will cause them to spoil if frozen raw.
- Leftovers should be cooled to room temperature or below before vacuum sealing to limit the risk of bacterial growth.

Be sure to mark all frozen food packages with the date and rotate items into use in the same way you do shelf-stable goods.

Dehydration

Dehydration is a simple food preservation method that creates shelf-stable product that is compact and storable in a smaller amount of space than the same food preserved in a different method. The only thing to consider with dehydrated food is that it uses a substantial amount of water to rehydrate the food, which can be an issue in situations during which water is scarce.

There are lots of ways to dehydrate food, and we'll discuss three of them here: commercial dehydrators, the oven, and off-grid methods. You can dehydrate fruits, vegetables, and meat. Regardless of the method, the preparation of the food will be the same.

Dehydration methods

Dehydrating using a commercial dehydrator: Since commercial dehydrators are designed to dehydrate, they're probably

---

*http://www.foodsaver.com/service-and-support/product-support/product
-faqs/food-science-and-safety/dos-and-donts/food-science-and-safety-dos
-and-donts-faq.html

the easiest, most effective method for dehydrating your food. When choosing a dehydrator, go with the best one that you can afford. On the lower end, the Nesco is a good brand. On the higher end, Excalibur is the hands-down champion.

The goal is to remove the moisture as quickly as possible. For fruits and vegetables, the ideal temperature for this is 130–140°F, with air circulating through the dehydrator. For best results, put the dehydrator in a dry area of your home, rather than a humid place like a basement or laundry room.

There are many variables when using a dehydrator that make it impossible to give specific times for drying foods. Variances like the power of your dehydrator, the amount of air circulation within, the juiciness of the specific food you're drying, and the ambient humidity can all affect the amount of time it takes to get the food to the proper amount of dryness.

Dehydrating using your oven: If you don't have a dehydrator, you can use your oven to dehydrate food if it has a setting that allows for a temperature below 150°F. Oven drying is much slower than drying with a dehydrator because it doesn't have a fan to circulate the air. Because it could take up to 24–48 hours to properly dry a batch of food for long-term storage, this could be a very inefficient method, particularly when heating up your house in the midst of summer.

To dehydrate food in your oven, prepare it as you would for the dehydrator. Place it on baking sheets and set the oven to 140°F. After the first two hours, crack the oven door to allow moisture to escape. Check for dryness using the methods above.

Dehydrating off grid: You can also harness the power of the summer sun to dry your food. Who hasn't seen a sunny farmhouse window with herbs hanging to dry?

For the best results, you need bright, sunny weather, temperatures of 100°F or greater, and very low humidity. This means that the desert is an ideal setting, but the Deep South, the Pacific Northwest, or the tropics probably won't be your best bet for drying food outdoors.

To dry fruits and vegetables outdoors, you will need to create a system that keeps the insects away. Mesh screens like you use for your windows are a good system.

You can create a drying rack system by placing one mesh screen with your produce topped by another mesh screen. Place these in a frame that allows for air circulation all the way around them.

Leave them outside in the sun during the day and pull them inside at night to keep them out of the nighttime dew or precipitation. Depending on your weather, it will take anywhere from 2–4 days to dry food completely outside.

Dehydrating Herbs

Probably the easiest and fastest thing to dehydrate is herbs. You can use your oven or your dehydrator, but be sure to put them on the very lowest possible setting or delicate herbs will burn.

I generally hang my herbs indoors in a sunny, warm place. A screen porch, solarium, or sunny window is ideal. Herbs will take anywhere from a couple of days to a week to dry completely. When they're dry, you can package them in glass jars for future use.

You can crumble them, store them as whole leaves, or powder them.

Dehydrating Fruits and Vegetables

Dehydrating fruits and vegetables is a simple, shelf-stable way to expand your pantry while taking up less space than storing the hydrated counterparts.

- Select good quality fruits and vegetables. Make sure they're ripe, and cut out any blemishes, soft spots, or bruises.
- If you have soft fruit or vegetables that you want to dehydrate, cut out any bad spots and then puree them to make fruit leather. For a bump in nutrition, you can mix in a *small* amount of mild-flavored pureed vegetables (like spinach) to add to very flavorful fruit. Think of it like a dehydrated version of smoothie.
- Wash your produce carefully, using baking soda to scrub skins on tougher items, and making a baking soda soak for delicate items. It's important to remove the pesticide and any residual chemicals, not only because they're bad for you, but because the flavor of them will be intensified during the dehydration process.
- Cut your produce into similar sizes to ensure uniform drying.
- Use acids like lemon juice to reduce browning of light-colored produce like apples and pears.
- Cruciferous vegetables like broccoli, cauliflower, or cabbage should be lightly blanched before dehydrating for best results.
- If you shred vegetables like squash or zucchini, salt it lightly, then put it in a colander over a pot in the fridge overnight to let it drain.

After drying, whatever method you opt for, use the following steps to ensure food safety.

- To test food for sufficient dryness, allow it to cool completely. Vegetables should be dry enough to snap, and fruits should be pliable and similar to leather in texture. Remember in the food storage section how we discussed botulism in an oxygen-free environment? Dehydrated food that retains some moisture that is then put into a container with the oxygen removed is a prime breeding ground for botulism.
- Fruit retains a bit more moisture than vegetables and it can be harder to tell if it is completely dry. It has to be "conditioned." Pack fruit pieces loosely in a glass jar for about 4–6 days before packing for the long-term. Give it a shake each day to redistribute any remaining moisture. If the jar builds up condensation, the fruit is not dry enough and needs to go back into the dehydrator.
- For foods that will be eaten quickly (like fruit roll-ups—they never last more than a few days in my house) it is fine if they

retain a bit more moisture. If they will be around for more than a day or two, store them in the refrigerator to inhibit the possibility of mold.

Storing Dehydrated Vegetables and Fruits

The National Center for Food Preservation* offers guidelines for safely storing your carefully dehydrated goodies.

- Allow the food to cool completely. When warm food cools, it can cause condensation. In a closed environment, this moisture creates a perfect habitat for mold to grow.
- Before packaging fruit for storage, be sure to condition it as described above.
- Store food in insect-proof containers like:
  - Canning jars
  - Plastic bags placed in another container
  - Freezer containers with lids that close airtight
- If you have a Foodsaver with a jar attachment, you can use this to vacuum seal your mason jars full of dried food. Be absolutely sure the food is totally dry before using this method—remember all of those warnings about botulism? Vacuum-packing creates an oxygen-free environment.
- For ultimate freshness, store your dehydrated foods in recipe-sized servings. This way you aren't opening and closing containers and introducing air or bacteria into your preserved food.
- Store your dehydrated food in a cool, dry, dark place.
- An environment that is humid can begin to rehydrate food, increasing the risk of spoilage and mold. The NCFP recommends glass jars for storing dehydrated food because it's visually obvious when moisture is introduced due to the visible condensation on the walls of the jars.

---

*http://nchfp.uga.edu/how/dry/pack_store.html

Reconstituting Dehydrated Produce

When it's time to use your dehydrated food, a little prep is sometimes necessary. Fruits are often enjoyed in their dried states, but when used in a recipe will need to be rehydrated. Vegetables are nearly always rehydrated, but one way to get around the soaking process is to add them to a pot of soup.

For foods that you intend to soak, use hot water and drain them thoroughly when they have plumped back up to their original state. A few more delicate foods reconstitute better with cold water. As a rule of thumb, use a ratio of 1 part food to 2 parts water. Err on the side of too much water.

Another way to make your dehydrated food tastier is to soak it in something other than water. Try broth, stock, or juice (for fruit).

You can usually tell by looking when the dried goodies have reached rehydration but the list below gives some commonly dehydrated foods and their soaking times.

- Broccoli: 15 minutes
- Cabbage: 60 minutes
- Carrots:* 30 minutes
- Corn: 30 minutes
- Green beans: 60 minutes
- Mushrooms:* 30 minutes
- Onions: 15 minutes
- Peas: 30 minutes
- Peppers: 20 minutes
- Spinach: 15 minutes
- Sweet potatoes: 30 minutes
- Tomatoes*: 30 minutes
- Zucchini: 30 minutes

A * indicates foods that are best when rehydrated with cold or room temperature water. This is because these foods are a little more delicate and rehydration with hot water could turn them into mush.

Methods for Preserving Meat

The preservation of meat is something that must be undertaken with great care. In my family, we freeze and can meat. (You can find specific how-tos for canning in the next section.) I'm not 100% comfortable with other methods of preservation, from a lack of personal experience with smoking, salting, and curing, and because of the warnings issued by the USDA regarding dehydrating. It's difficult to find a consensus on the shelf life of meat preserved by dehydrating, curing, or smoking, so if you plan to preserve meat in one of these ways, do a lot of research and learn from an expert if you can. The shelf life of dried meat in particular is highly debated. Personally, I don't use home-dried meats and instead, purchase freeze-dried meats from reputable sources. My hesitance in using it for my own family and my personal inexperience precludes me from putting instructions for dehydrating meat in this book.

Curing, salting, and smoking meats are age-old arts, but these are not projects I've undertaken, so again, I'll leave the specific instructions to the experts. If you opt to use one of these methods, please learn from a reliable source. Foodborne illness is the last thing you'll want to face when you are in a situation during which you must rely on your pantry.

Canning meat

One of my favorite ways to preserve meat is home-canning. Once you try home-canned chicken or beef, you'll never settle for those unpleasant little grocery store tins of bits and pieces again.

A pressure canner is a necessity for safely preserving low-acid foods. Meat of any type is low-acid, so *must* be pressure canned. Be sure to check a canning book (like mine, *The Prepper's Canning Guide*) for specific times and pressures for processing meat. Nearly all meats should be processed in a pressure canner for 90 minutes, using a pressure of 10 pounds at sea level. If you are at a higher elevation, the necessary pressure will increase. Complete instructions for using a pressure canner can be found in the canning section of this book.

There is an old canning adage that says, "When in doubt, throw it out." Nowhere in Canning-land is that more true than with home-canned meat. Be sure your jars have sealed properly, and if you discover a jar on your shelf that has come unsealed, discard it where no family members or animals can get to it. This could be a sign of botulism, which can cause permanent impairment or death. (Is anyone sick of hearing about botulism yet? Sorry, it's a very real concern with storage food, and awareness is a vital step in prevention.)

You can find lots of great canning recipes for meat preservation. Preserve small roasts, ground meat with seasoning, soups, stews, or chili. Canned meat is melt-in-your-mouth tender from the high pressure processing. My kids absolutely love it. You know a food storage method is a success when your children are sad when opening the last jar.

Freezing meat

In an earlier section, we discussed freezing in specific detail. This is one of the most popular methods for preserving meat. Use a vacuum sealer to repackage your meat for best results.

The only drawback to using your freezer to store meat is that in the event of a power outage, the loss could be great. Often, home-owner's insurance will reimburse you for a portion of the freezer items lost in an extended outage, but you will have a smelly, disgusting mess to deal with unless the food is discarded immediately, before it has time to rot. I once had a freezer that got unplugged in the basement. We discovered it a few weeks later when a horrible smell began emanating from the storage area below us. The freezer itself was beyond cleaning and had to be discarded, contents and all. Ugh. Trust me, if the food is spoiled during a power outage, deal with it immediately.

Dehydrating meat

One way some families add shelf-stable meat to their stockpile is to dehydrate it. This must be undertaken carefully in order to be safe, but the process is really very simple. When most people think of dried meat, they think about jerky. However, people dehydrate all sorts of meat and use it in recipes. Remember that rehydration can use up valuable water supplies. Use rehydrated meat in things like casseroles, soups, and sauces, where the consistency isn't as important.

Curing, Smoking, and Salting Meat

If you want to go old school, learn one of these low-tech ways to preserve meat without the need for refrigeration. They can be done completely off-grid, making them particularly applicable to a long-term power outage situation.

Cured, smoked, and salted meat can last for a very long time when prepared properly. If you intend to use these methods for preserving food, you will need to stock up on curing salt, which is a different compound than table salt.

Canning

One of the best ways to build your healthy stockpile is to preserve local organic foods when they are in season. My favorite way to do this is canning. I love canning so much that I wrote an entire book about it. So, this frugal, creative, and delicious food preservation section will be a little longer while I wax poetic.

When you can your own food, you can make delicious entrees and side dishes that can be served as quickly as you can boil water—and the best part of all is that you know exactly what is in those shiny jars. In the event of a power outage, not having to cook food from scratch is a huge benefit, as it saves on fuel and, in the worst-case scenario, you can eat the food straight from the jar without heating it up.

Making home-canned foods can be a great way to cost-effectively build your pantry for several reasons:

- You can buy in bulk
- You can take advantage of good sales, like "last day" sales
- You can buy what is in season at better prices than when it is out of season
- You can put together "quick meals" far less expensively than buying processed foods by doing a big batch of home cooking to be reheated and eaten at a later date
- You don't risk losing your stockpile to the vagaries of the power grid like you would by using your freezer

When my daughter eats a biscuit with jam, I know that jam only contains organic peaches and sugar. There are no GMOs lurking, no high fructose corn syrup, and no artificial colors and flavors.

Lots of meals for very little money
You can get a lot of bang for your buck by home canning. I recently canned some "meals in a jar"—check out what I spent:

$10 = 7 quart jars of spaghetti sauce with meatballs
$4 = 6 quart jars of Boston baked beans

If you were to purchase those items in grocery store cans you'd be spending far more money for far less quality.

One week I concentrated on building my pantry with home-canned goods. I purchased items specifically for this purpose.

I made:

- **7 half-pints of jalapeno relish**
- **3 pints of brown sugar peach preserves**
- **4 half-pints of jalapeno peach jam**
- **7 quart jars of spaghetti sauce with meatballs**
- **6 quart jars of Boston baked beans**
- **4 pints of wild blackberry jam**
- **4 quarts of pinto beans with bacon**

I made all of the above for about $35, not including snap lids and spices, which only add nominally to the cost.

Here are some ways to save money by canning:

1. **Don't decide ahead of time what you are going to can.** It's okay to have a general idea, but if you have specific recipes that require specific ingredients beyond your pantry basics, you may end up spending a lot of money. For example, yesterday I went to a garden exchange and swapped some money and some home-canned goodies for other people's surplus produce. When I got the items home, I took a look at my bounty and decided what to make based on that. Had I gone to the store or market specifically looking for certain things, I would have spent far more.

2. **Always fill your canner.** If you only have enough ingredients for 5 jars of whatever you're making, but your pressure canner holds 7 jars, fill the other two jars with beans. You're using the same amount of electricity or gas whether the canner is full or not.

3. **Buy as much as you can when things are inexpensive.** Check out your local orchard. They often sell bushel and half-bushel sized boxes for a fraction of the price of getting your fruit in smaller quantities.

4. **Cook in bulk and can your leftovers.** The holidays can supply an enormous amount of ingredients for your home canning endeavors. Also, as the weather cools off, make double batches of chili, soups, and stews and put the leftovers into jars for later use.

5. **Learn to can with what you have on hand.** Going along with tip #1, be flexible and learn to adapt the ingredients you have on hand in canning.

Canning is easy!

If you've never canned before, there's no time like the present to learn how! For a very small investment you can begin water bath canning, and once you have the hang of that, you can make the larger (but much more versatile) investment into a pressure canner.

Following, you'll find a quick introduction to canning.

Canning 101: Jar Prep

Your preserved food is only as safe and sanitary as the vessels you put it into. An important step that must not be overlooked is sanitizing and preparing the jars, lids, and rings. There are several methods for this.

The dishwasher method

If you have a dishwasher, this is easy. Just run it on the sanitizing cycle right before you begin canning. The dishwasher will keep the jars hot until you are ready to fill them. The heat from the dishwasher will also make the rubber on the jar flat more pliable and ready to seal.

The water bath canner method

Assuming that your jars are clean and all you need to do is sterilize them, you can use your water bath canner for this. (This is the method I use, since I no longer have a dishwasher.) Place the jars in the canner, on the rack. Pour in enough water that it goes over the openings of the jars and fills them. Bring the canner to a boil and allow it to boil for 10 minutes. Then use your jar lifter and remove the jars, placing them upside down on a towel or drying rack to drain. You can reuse the hot water for canning once the jars are filled and lidded.

The Oven Method

You can also use your oven to sterilize your jars. Preheat your oven to 225°F. Place your jars in a roasting pan and slide them into the oven for at least 20 minutes. At that point, you can turn off the heat, but leave the jars in there until they are ready to be packed.

Warning: (this is kind of a "duh" but I'll say it anyway!) The jars will be hotter than heck when you take them out of the oven—take care not to burn yourself when filling them and placing them in the canner! Sometimes I use this method—when I do, I leave the jars in the roasting pan while I fill them and then use my jar lifter to move them from the roasting pan to the canner.

Sanitizing the Lids

In a small saucepan, bring to a simmer enough water to cover your flats and rings. Do not bring the flats to a rolling boil, as this could damage the sealing compound. Keep the lids in the hot water and remove them with sterilized tongs or a lid lifter (a cool little magnetic wand) when you are ready to put them on the jars.

*   *   *

Sometimes all of the canning rules sound overwhelming! Please don't let them scare you. I'm providing you with the best practices so that you have all the information you need.

Keep in mind that you are not performing open-heart surgery. Nearly all canning recipes have to be processed for more than 10 minutes, which, in conjunction with the presterilization you have performed, should help you to keep your food safe and healthy.

Canning 101: Water Bath Canning

Water bath canning is a great way to get going for beginners. There is no scary equipment, the start-up cost is minimal, and there is less margin for error.

Water bath canning is a safe method for preserving high-acid foods. Some examples of foods that can be canned in a water bath are:

- Jams and jellies
- Fruit
- Applesauce
- Pickles
- Tomato products

For water bath canning you must have the following tools:

- Big canning pot
- Rack (if you don't have a rack you can use a folded towel in the bottom of the pot)

- Jar lifter
- Jar funnel (not absolutely necessary but it really reduces waste and mess)

These items are the minimum tools you need for canning properly and safely. There are all sorts of other gadgets out there, like items that help you measure headspace and lid lifters with a little magnet on the end, but if you have the above items—you are ready to can!

Then, of course, you need:

- Jars
- Flats (also called snap lids)
- Rings

Step-by-Step
While your product is simmering away . . .

1. **Sanitize your jars, lids, and rings**. We talked about this already.
2. **Prepare your canner**. Place your rack in the bottom of your canner and fill your canner with water, leaving about 3–5 inches at the top to allow for room for your filled jars. If you don't have a rack, you can line the bottom with a folded towel. Bring your water to a boil. Because it takes forever and a day to bring that much water to a boil, I generally start it while I am prepping my food.
3. **Fill your jars**. Line up your jars on a heat-proof surface near the stove. You can place a towel on the counter to protect it from the hot, filled jars. Using the funnel, ladle the prepared product into the jars, leaving the headspace recommended in your recipe.
4. **Put on your lids**. With a dry, clean dishtowel, carefully wipe the lip of the filled jars, removing any residue. Place the flats on each jar, then finger tighten the rings. You don't

have to really torque on them—the job of the rings it to hold the flats in place until they seal.

5. **Place your jars in the canner**. With your handy-dandy jar lifter, place the closed jars carefully into the canner. Put them in gently so that boiling water doesn't splash on you. Be careful not to let the jars touch because they could break when they bump together in the boiling water. Make sure the lids are all completely submerged under the water. They don't have to be under by inches—just covered.

6. **Process the jars**. Put the lid back on and return the canner back to a rolling boil. Don't start clocking your processing time until the water is at a full boil. Then just leave the jars in the water bath for the amount of time required in your recipe. If you want to sound productive you can refer to this as "processing your jars."

7. **Remove the jars from the canner**. Using your jar lifter, carefully remove the jars from the boiling water. Tip the jars to the side to allow the hot water to drip off the top. Then place the jar on your towel or heat-proof surface.

8. **Now, leave them alone!** Allow 12–24 hours for the jars to cool and seal. You will hear a musical "plink" noise as the jars seal in the cool air—that is the lid getting sucked down and forming a seal to the lip of the jar.

When you are ready to store the jars, you can remove the rings. This keeps your rings from rusting because of moisture trapped between the metal ring and the jar. Test the seal by pushing down with your finger. If it pops back and forth it is not sealed. Put it in the refrigerator and use the unsealed product in the next few days. Store the sealed jars in a cool, dark place.

Canning 101: Pressure Canning

First, here are a few words of encouragement about pressure canning.

Number one, you are NOT going to blow yourself up. Let's put this thought to rest right now! My first attempt at pressure canning took place after I'd sent the girls off to school one day, just in case things began exploding. I had anxious visions of geysers of boiling water, a hole in the ceiling where the lid of the canner had flown off, and third-degree burns. I was a nervous wreck!

It was sort of a non-event, to be quite honest. There are some loud noises to get used to, it's a bit alarming to put a stopper on the steam coming out of the little vent on top, and you have to patiently wait for the pressure to reduce at the end.

There are only a few ways that you are likely to hurt yourself or blow up your kitchen (and even then, it's really, really unlikely, particularly with the new canners and all their requisite safety measures):

- You use equipment that is old and faulty.
- You can something when the vent is blocked (peek through and check it each time—takes 2 seconds!).
- You allow the pressure to exceed 17 PSI and you leave it like that for an extended period of time.
- You try to remove the lid before the pressure has dispersed.

If you don't do any of those things, you will be perfectly safe—I promise! Always read your manufacturer's instructions, and if those instructions differ from mine, FOLLOW THEIRS! They are the experts on their own equipment.

Low-acid foods have to be preserved at a higher temperature than high-acid foods. Pressure canning exceeds the temperature of water bath canning, getting your product into the safety zone. The temperature must reach 240°F, which can only be achieved through steam under pressure.

All vegetables (except for tomatoes which are botanically a fruit), meats, seafood, and poultry must be preserved in a pressure canner.

Lots of people like to say, "Well, my grandmother never used a pressure canner and she canned these without one. We never died, so I am going to do the same thing."

Previous generations also held their babies on their laps in the front seat of the car, allowed their children to stand in the back of the pick-up, and many other things that we don't currently consider to be safe. It's simply not worth the risk to your family members' lives to save $200 investment in proper equipment. **If you don't want to use a pressure canner, please do not can low-acid foods**.

For pressure canning you need:

- Pressure canner with valves, seals, and gauges
- Rack (if you don't have a rack you can use a folded towel in the bottom of the pot)
- Jar lifter
- Jar funnel

As with water bath canning, you can get all the extra gadgets if you want too, but these are the essentials.

Step-by-Step

One thing you will notice about pressure canning is that nearly all of the steps are identical to the method for water bath canning. Differences are really only related to the equipment. So, once you have learned to use your pressure canner correctly, you will find it every bit as easy as water bath canning.

1. **You don't have to sanitize your jars, lids, and rings**. Just make sure they're clean and that will be sufficient. The pressure and length of processing time will ensure safety.

2. **Prepare your canner.** Place your rack or folded towel in the bottom of your canner add about 3 inches of water to the canner. Most p-canners have a line to which you fill the water. In pressure canning it is not necessary for the water to cover the lids. (Always check the instructions on your individual canner—it there is a discrepancy, go with the instructions that came with your product.) At this point, you can turn the burner on low to begin warming the water, but don't bring it to a boil yet.

3. **Fill your jars**. Line up your jars on the counter near the stove. If the surface is not heat-proof, place a towel on the counter first because the filled jars will be very hot. Using the funnel, ladle the prepared product into the jars, leaving the headspace recommended in your recipe.

4. **Put on your lids**. With a dry, clean dishtowel, carefully wipe the lip of the filled jars, making sure to get any residue of food off. Place the flats on each jar, then finger tighten the rings—you don't have to really torque on them.

5. **Place your jars in the canner.** Place the closed jars into the canner. Be careful not to let the jars touch because not only could they could break when they bump together in the boiling water, but in p-canning the steam must be able to completely circulate around the jars.

6. **Build steam in the canner.** Before putting the lid on the canner, check the vent pipe every single time to be sure it is clear. Place the lid firmly on the canner, latching it as per the specifics of your canner, and increase the heat to bring the water to a boil. At this point steam should be coming out the

vent pipe. Reduce the heat until a moderate amount of steam is coming steadily out the pipe for 10 minutes. The purpose of this is to release the air and build up the steam inside the canner. If you don't give it the whole 10 minutes, your canner will not build pressure. As patience is not my strong point, I learned this from experience.

7. **Close the vent.** After exhausting the steam for 10 minutes, depending on your canner, either close the petcock or place the weighted regulator on the vent pipe. When I place the regulator on, I always put a dishtowel around my hand, because, yeah, steam is HOT. It sometimes makes a loud high-pitched noise when you are putting the regulator on—I scared myself the first time and screamed, causing my child to think I'd gone and blown myself up. (Teehee.) Don't be alarmed by the various rattling, whistling, and bubbling noises. P-canning is loud business.

8. **Pressurize the canner.** Turn up the heat on the burner and wait until the gauge has reached the desired pressure. (Pressure will differ based on altitudes and recipes). This usually takes 3–5 minutes. Note: if you lose pressure during processing you must restart the processing time. Adjust the heat to maintain the pressure—this takes practice. Monitor your canner throughout the processing time to be sure the pressure is maintained. I have found that approximately #4 on the dial on my electric stove keeps my pressure between 10–12 pounds quite steadily.

9. **Release the pressure.** When your processing time is over it is time to release the pressure. It couldn't be easier. Turn off the burner. Take the canner off the burner and put it on a heat-proof surface. Walk away. Allow the canner to return to room temperature and release pressure naturally. Don't try to do anything to cool it down faster—that is how people get hurt p-canning. Pressure is completely reduced when the air vent/cover lock and overpressure plug have dropped and no steam escapes when the pressure regulator is tilted. The

gauge, if your canner has one, should be completely at zero. This can take 45 minutes to an hour and cannot be rushed!

10. **Open the vent.** When pressure is gone, open the petcock or remove the weighted regulator. If the regulator doesn't want to come off, there is likely still some pressure in the canner. Don't force it. Walk away for another 15 minutes. Once the vent is open, leave the canner for another 2–5 minutes.

11. **Remove the jars from the canner.** Use potholders to protect your hands while you unlatch the lid of your p-canner. Very carefully remove the lid to the canner, facing it away from you so that you are not burned by the steam that will rush out. Using your jar lifter, carefully remove the jars from the canner, one by one. Then place the jars on your towel or heat-proof surface.

12. **Allow 12–24 hours for the jars to cool and seal.** Let the jars stand in a draft-free place without being moved or bumped, usually overnight. Jars that are sealed properly will bubble away on the counter for quite some time after they are removed from the p-canner. You will hear a musical "pop" as the jars seal in the cool air—that is the lid getting sucked down and forming a seal on the jar. When you are ready to store the jars, you can remove the rings and then test the seal by pushing down with your finger. If it pops back and forth it is not sealed. Put it in the refrigerator and use the unsealed product right away. Store your sealed jars in a cool, dark place.

I have tons and tons of recipes for both pressure canning and water bath canning in my book, *The Prepper's Canning Guide.*

Canning 101: Adjusting for Altitude

It's all science, like so much of canning is. At sea level, and up to 1000 feet above sea level, water boils at 212°F.

However, once you get above the 1000-foot mark, the changes in atmospheric pressure mean that your boiling point is actually LOWER than 212°F.

Altitude	Temperature at which water boils
10,000	194°F
8,000	197°F
6,000	201°F
4,000	204°F
2,000	208°F
0 (Sea Level)	212°F

For water bath canning, food safety requirements mean that the goodies inside your jars should reach 212°F, and if it doesn't you have to add to your processing time in order to make your preserved food safe.

For water bath canning, add 2 minutes of processing time for each 1000 feet above 1000 feet that you are. To use the following chart, take the basic processing time and add to it based on your local elevation.

Altitude Adjustments for Water Bath Canning	
Elevation	+ time
1000–2999	5 minutes
3000–5999	10 minutes
6000–7999	15 minutes
8000–10,000	20 minutes

Pressure canning requires that your food reach 240°F. Additional pressure is needed in this case, as opposed to additional time. The standard rule is to add 1 pound of pressure for each 1000 feet above sea level you are. However, you will rarely ever adjust more than 5 pounds, regardless of your elevation.

For safety reasons, pressure canners should never be used above 17 pounds of pressure.

Adjustments for Pressure Canning	
Altitude	Additional Pressure
1001–2000	+ 1
2001–4000	+ 3
4001–6000	+ 5
6001–8000	+ 5
8001–10,000	+ 5

A few words of warning

Please use the currently-approved canning practices described here.

This does not mean "oven canning" or "heat it up and then turn the jar upside-down" canning. It doesn't mean water bath canning meat for three hours.

It's not worth it to take these risky short cuts that honestly aren't even that much shorter.

If you don't want to use the safest possible methods of canning, I strongly advise that you choose other methods of food preservation.

Where to Stash Your Stockpile

Stockpiles: they aren't just for pantries anymore!

You might be wondering where on earth you can stash all of the food required for a one-year pantry. Unless you have a pantry the size of a master bedroom suite, it won't take long to exceed the limits of your available kitchen storage.

Storage Rooms

If you're really lucky, you'll have an entire room that you can commit to your pantry supplies. The beauty of a room in your house is that it is likely to be far more temperature stable than a basement, attic, or storage shed. You can have an organized storeroom, full of neatly labeled shelves.

When shopping for shelving for a storage area, don't skimp on quality. Buying cheap shelves will do you little good when they collapse under the weight of the food you put on them.

I prefer industrial shelving because it's sturdy and rated for weight. You can get attractive wire shelving units rated for 500 pounds per shelf, or heavy-duty steel shelving rated for 1000

pounds per shelf. Some discount stores have heavy plastic shelves that are very simple to snap together that will hold 50–100 pounds per shelf. Purchase the best quality, sturdiest shelves that you can afford. If your budget is tight, consider a combination of these shelves for storing different types of items.

For shelves in the center of the room (not backed up against the wall and anchored) look for wide, low shelving for extra stability.

Place the heaviest items (like buckets) on the bottom shelves, and work up to lighter items on higher shelves.

The All-Over-the-House Pantry

If you don't have a storage room that looks like something from Pinterest, don't despair. Most of us *don't*!

There are lots of little nooks, crannies, and storage areas around most homes that will allow you to discreetly put away a year's supply of food for your family. Even those who dwell in apartments or other small spaces might be surprised to discover how many little hidden areas they actually have.

When you store things in different places throughout the house, it's important to store like items together and to document your organizational efforts with a "map." Without this guideline, you may find yourself wasting valuable time searching for a package of flour that you know you packed away or repurchasing items that you already have, but just can't find.

Get organized!

Set aside a day (or weekend) to get organized. This is a big, messy undertaking, so choose a day where you won't be constantly interrupted and can work until you're finished.

1. Pull all of your preps into one room.
2. Separate them into like items: grains, paper products, baking supplies, jarred goods, etc. (This is a great time to update your inventory list with totals!)
3. Clean out your nooks and crannies in which you plan to stash away your items.
4. Make a map documenting where you store each item.
5. Put the food away, oldest items at the front.

Your "map" can also serve as a running inventory. It can be constantly updated with the amounts of items you are putting away and taking for use in the kitchen. If you plan to update like that, consider a dry-erase board hung on the inside of the pantry door.

Keeping your map on the computer is a great idea . . . unless the power goes down. It's important to have a hard copy for that reason.

Where Can You Store All of That Food?

Every room in the house is fair game. There's no reason that food must only be stored in the kitchen. Keep similar items together, for the sake of organization. Think about the grocery store—even in one where you've never shopped, it's generally easy to find items because similar things are organized together. There is a condiment aisle, a cereal aisle, etc. You can apply this principle to your home storage also.

Here are some places that I store preps in my home, along with ideas from previous places we have lived.

Kitchen pantry

Items currently in rotation live in the kitchen pantry. When these items get low, I rotate in their replacements from the other location.

Kitchen shelves

Home-canned foods—these will be eaten within a year of preserving them, so I keep them handy. Plus, I love the old-fashioned look of the jars. Everyone knows I can, so this doesn't bring any undue attention.

Broom closet

I installed shelves in this closet to make it easier to find things. Shelf 1: food buckets with Mylar bags of food inside. Shelf 2: Cleaning supplies, dish soap. Shelf 3: Candles, lighters, extra solar lights, matches, lamp oil, batteries. Shelf 4: Tools, screws, nails, and other small hardware.

Blanket storage area in guest room
Beans. Bags and bags and bags of beans that have been sealed into Mylar bags.

Armoire in guest room
"Decorative" boxes (I glued attractive paper to the outside of regular cardboard boxes and edged them with ribbon) full of baking items like baking soda, baking powder, chocolate chips, etc.

Mudroom
5-gallon water jugs, laundry supplies, hardware, food buckets with Mylar bags of food inside.

Basement
1-gallon water jugs of tap water, canned goods purchased from the store, root cellar items, shampoo, conditioner, laundry products, bath products, cleaning supplies.

Notice that none of these things will spoil easily if exposed to humidity. Basements can be damp, so they are not a good place for paper goods or other items that would be negatively affected by moisture.

Garage
Extra 5-gallon jugs of drinking water, pet food in airtight Rubbermaid-style containers, food buckets with Mylar bags of food inside, food from LDS cannery. Garages can have widely fluctuating temperatures depending on your climate and how well-insulated they are, so choose what goes into your garage accordingly.

Attic
Paper goods like toilet paper, paper towels, paper plates; garbage bags; baby wipes. These are stored in Rubbermaid-style containers

to prevent rodents from nesting in paper goods. Be careful storing any items that might be heat sensitive in an attic.

Laundry room closet

Buckets of bulk grains, floor to ceiling. I wrote on the front of the buckets with a permanent marker for ease in finding the grain I'm looking for.

Laundry room shelf

Laundry supplies, grocery store canned goods in a single row all the way to the top behind the laundry supplies.

Living room bookcases

There is a pretty curtain running in front of the bottom shelf. Behind the curtain are dozens of jugs of white vinegar, as well as balsamic vinegar, apple cider vinegar, and red wine vinegar.

Linen closet

Grocery store canned meats (we never use these and they exist as a last resort), fruit, dry milk, and pie filling. Medicines and first aid supplies.

Bedroom closets

The back wall is lined with boxed goods like cereal, crackers, etc. There is a cool bungee cord grid holding the boxes in place.

Under beds

I filled those little rolling under-bed containers with dry pet food. Also under the beds are things like toilet paper and individual water bottles in cases.

Storage furniture

Due to homes getting smaller and budgets getting tighter, lots of furniture comes with storage built right in: coffee tables, end tables, nightstands, beds, ottomans—some couches even have a storage area under the cushions. This can help you to make the most of your space with hidden mini-pantries all through the house.

Pick up decorative antique trunks and luggage at yard sales and thrift stores and make them part of your décor, secretly stashing all manner of supplies in them.

Outbuildings

Barns, sheds, and summerhouses can all provide abundant space. However, the same rules that apply for garages apply for other outbuildings. Beware of extremes in temperature, moisture, and rodents and other pests.

When coming home from a shopping trip, I always put the new supplies away in the correct spot, rotating the older items to the front. Each week I "shop" the food storage and rotate needed items into the kitchen. Since I've begun doing it this way, I have never run into the issue of having preps slip through the expiration date cracks, nor have I had to dig through anything to find a needed item!

Prepper OPSEC 101

It is important to maintain your OPSEC when stashing away your food. OPSEC is a term swiped from the military that means OPerational SECurity. It means that your operations, in this case, your one-year supply of food, should not be public knowledge.

OPSEC is the process of protecting little pieces of data that could be grouped together to give the bigger picture.

In the event of a long-term disaster, your neighborhood will be filled with hungry people. Even in a short-term disaster, as we saw in the aftermath of Hurricane Sandy, some people were without food after only 2–3 days. You don't want your home to be known as the one with all the food. During an event that results in civil unrest, you could become a target.

For this reason, you don't want to store your goods out in the open. Discretion is key. Hungry folks have long memories, and they will recall if you have a kitchen or hallway that is stacked to the raf-ters with food buckets or canned goods.

This is also a benefit to storing your food in various places around the house. In the unfortunate event that your food is stolen, it is pos-sible that only a portion of your food will be taken. The thieves may not think to also check your basement, under your bed, and in the laundry room. Some preppers even keep a dummy stash of food that they are willing to give up in such an event, while the bulk of their items remain hidden safely away.

Efficient Use of the Stockpile

Congratulations! After months of careful budgeting, shopping, food preservation, repackaging, and stockpiling, you now have a one-year food supply.

This doesn't mean that you don't have to shop for a year, but it does mean that you have a cushion against disaster, whether it be personal, regional, financial, or natural. It gives you the freedom to wait out price spikes and purchase items on sale or in bulk. It means fewer trips to the store (and less temptation to go off-budget). It means that when scanning new recipes you nearly always have the ingredients on hand to make the delicious goodies that you find.

Once you've built your pantry, you have to develop a plan to maintain it. You don't want to end up back at square one a year from now!

Using Your Stockpiled Items

First of all, remember that you bought this food to eat. While some items might be stored for many years in case of a dire, long-term emergency, most of these foods should be rotated into your kitchen and replaced as needed.

- To reiterate, when you store your foods, always place the oldest items with the closest expiry dates at the front. Place newly purchased items at the back.

- Before your grocery shopping trips, check your pantry first. Do you have home-canned goods that need to be eaten? Is there a bag of pasta that is nearing expiration? Work those into your menu plan before shopping.

- Speaking of menu planning, decide ahead of time what you plan to serve that week. You may discover that you actually need very few items, freeing up your budget for sale purchases that replenish your stockpile.

- When your stockpile is properly maintained, your weekly purchases should only be for fresh produce and dairy products. The remainder of your budget can go to make large buys of sale items with which to replenish your pantry. Use your stockpile for the basics like pasta, meat, baking supplies, and soups.

Maintaining Your One-Year Pantry

Once you've created your pantry, it is important to maintain it. You don't want to deplete your food stockpile without a plan to replenish it. Although items that you purchase seasonally will drop throughout the year, you need to maintain a certain level of pantry basics.

- Keep a running inventory. If you don't know what you have, you don't know what you need. I created an Excel document on my computer for this. Some people keep a clipboard in the pantry with a printed list that they update when they take items for kitchen use.

- When staple items drop to a certain point, begin looking for a good deal.

- Stockpile seasonally. During harvest season, focus on preserving fresh fruits and vegetables for later in the year. In the winter spend your money on grain items and pantry basics purchased in large quantities. In the fall, make bulk meat purchases, like a half cow or half pig.

- Track the sales cycles throughout the year in order to purchase staples when they are at the lowest prices. There is a very distinct and predictable pattern to these good buys. For example, baking supplies nearly always go on sale just before Christmas, canned goods drop in February, etc.

- Keep a price book to help you track the cost of various items in your area. This will help you to know whether a deal is as good as it is promoted to be. Stockpile shopping, when done right, can save you a fortune in annual food costs.

- Pay attention to your repackaging practices. Your purchases are only as fresh as your storage methods There's nothing worse than grabbing something from your stockpile, only to find that it is stale or full of bugs. If your foods are not stored properly, your money has gone to waste.

Expand Your Stockpile Beyond Food

This book is about creating a food pantry. However, true preparedness has a much broader scope than simply keeping your family fed.

You don't have to limit your new strategies only to things that are edible.

You can apply your stockpile principle to save money on many other items, while also increasing your family's level of preparedness.

If some of these supplies seem frivolous, please remember that not all disasters are post-apocalyptic nuclear winters where the other survivors are trying to eat you. Sometimes, you just have money problems. In cases like that, you're still going to go to work, and the kids are still going to go to school, so being clean, comfortable, and well-groomed is just as important as it was before.

Here are a few examples of other stockpiles that we keep in our home.

- Shower gel
- Soap
- Laundry products
- Shampoo
- Conditioner
- Disposable razors
- Band-Aids
- First aid supplies
- Calamine lotion
- Dish soap
- Feminine hygiene items
- Toilet paper
- Paper towels
- Baby wipes (even if you don't have a baby!)
- Cosmetics
- Coconut oil
- Peroxide
- Rubbing alcohol
- Hand sanitizer
- Bleach
- White vinegar
- Cleaning supplies
- Garbage bags
- Kitty litter (for emergency sanitation AND cats)
- Pet food
- Flea and tick medication for pets
- Tea tree oil
- Lotion
- Sunscreen
- Extra filters for your water filtration device
- Spare parts for important equipment like canners or tools
- Matches
- Lighters
- Candles
- Batteries
- Stationery/school/office supplies

Your stockpile will save you time, money, and stress.

When you have a well-provisioned home, you can meet most situations with aplomb. Scenarios that would have other people scrambling to provide the basic necessities for their family will hardly register as a blip on your radar.

Prepping is the Ultimate Act of Optimism

How many times have you been called "gloomy" or "depressing?" How many times have others considered you pessimistic?

Does this sound familiar?

You're talking to a friend or family member who isn't on board with preparedness. (And it's even worse when they *think* they know what's going on in the world but garner their so-called "information" from network news sources.) You try for the millionth time to get them to consider stocking up on a few things and they shake their head and say, "Oh, please. Life's too short for all of this doom and gloom. Live a little! You are such a pessimist!"

My response to this is that *preparedness is the ultimate form of optimism.*

One who practices skills, makes dramatic lifestyle changes, and studies current events critically may come across to the uninitiated as a person who has buried himself or herself in negativity, but in fact, one who prepares is saying to life, "Whatever comes, we are not only going to live through it, my family is going to thrive, and I will not bend my knee to tyranny for an MRE and a bottle of water."

I think that methods of preparedness can be compared to love songs on the radio. Bear with me through this analogy.

If the songs that make you think of your significant other are sad, with reference to breaking up and getting back together, unsatisfied yearnings, arguments, frustration, anger, and broken hearts, you just might be doing the whole "love" thing wrong. Shouldn't the song that makes you think of the one you love be happy, upbeat, and full of joy? Shouldn't thoughts of that special someone make you more prone to goofy smiles and a warm glow than to melancholy longing or the urge to gleefully burn all of their belongings in a great pile in the front yard?

It's exactly the same with preparedness. Thoughts of your plans, your lifestyle, and your loaded pantry room should give you a sense of peace and security. If your state of preparedness makes you feel unhappy, stressed, angry, or resentful, you're doing something wrong.

Here are some examples of how prepping is pure, unadulterated optimism:

- Your area is under a severe storm warning. While everyone else you know is rushing to the store and knocking over old ladies to clear the shelves, you're tying down some outdoor furniture, filling the bathtubs with water, bringing in some extra firewood, cooking up some stuff that would be likely to go bad during an extended power outage, and getting the candles and lanterns ready. Perhaps you are discussing with your kids why you're doing what you're doing and using it as a teachable moment. There is no panic, only the peace of mind you feel when you don't have to try to get things that everyone else is trying to procure at the exact same frenzied moment.

- During this hypothetical storm, the power goes out for two weeks, water is under a boil order, and trees are down everywhere. You remain in the safety of your home with your family, not risking downed power lines and falling branches from storm-damaged trees. You heat up hearty meals using off-grid cooking methods with which you are already familiar. You spend the two-week break playing board games, reading books, doing art projects. You have plenty of food, plenty of water, and plenty of light. To your kids, this is an adventure and to you it's a little break from your regular work and from technology.

- Heaven forbid that you should lose your job, but if you did, you have the security of a supply of food to see you through. You know how to grow your own food to supplement this supply because you've been doing it for years. You know a million different ways to do things manually and save yourself money. While a loss of income is a crisis, for someone who has readied themselves for the possibility, it could also be an opportunity to seek a new job, to homeschool the kids, to start a business of their own. If they don't feel that horrible sense of desperation, realizing that the mortgage payment is coming out in three weeks, and they don't have the money to pay it, the utilities are already close to being cut off, and there are three slices of bread in the house, with two of them being the crusty heels that nobody wants to eat, then the person is a little more free to search for the silver lining.

- One fine summer day when you are enjoying a barbecue at a friend's house, you listen to other folks complaining about the cost of produce at the grocery store due to the droughts and poor growing conditions across the country. You realize that you haven't purchased a single vegetable since your spring lettuce and peas prolifically came in, and you had absolutely no idea that everyone else was paying double or triple what they paid last year for a bag of baby spinach or a pound of tomatoes.

- If someone you know falls on hard times, you are always able to lend a hand with a bag full of groceries that came directly from your pantry. You don't even have to think twice about helping out, because you are prepared for the long haul.

What non-preparedness people just can't seem to understand is that what we seek is peace of mind, freedom, and security for our families, not just a weekend at Disney World. We don't wish to delude ourselves with the soothing lies and distractions of the mainstream media so that we can blithely go about the business of trying to guess which B-list performer is going to take the crown (do they have a crown?) on *Dancing with the Stars*. We like reality, not reality TV, and we'd rather not have surprises. We can still have fun that doesn't compromise our ideals, sabotage our progress, or deter us from our paths.

We don't want to be lulled into a false sense of prosperity, hypnotized by our iPhones and our "smart" wristwatches, or pacified with governmental lies about the "economic recovery." We don't want to deal with the ill health that comes from eating substances that aren't even food but are guaranteed by the government to be "generally recognized as safe" (there's a glowing recommendation, huh?) or stumble through life in a fluoride-induced brain fog.

We just want to go out to our garden and get some unsprayed heirloom tomatoes, for crying out loud, and thrive on real food, clean water, and an avoidance of Big Pharma chemicals.

Here's a final analogy.

Imagine that you are out for a walk, and you get lost in the woods. You end up wandering around for a couple of days, and you're exhausted and hungry. You come upon two bushes, different varieties of plants, both with brightly colored berries.

- Would you rather know for certain that one of those bushes bears edible fruit that won't harm you, and consume those berries with confidence because you have taken the effort to be educated on the flora of the area?
- Or would you prefer to have absolutely no idea which one is safe because the thought that you might have to rely on berries in the woods to survive is pessimistic, and you refused to spoil a great hiking trip with negative thinking beforehand?

Preparedness: It means that whatever may come, you intend to not only grimly survive, but to thrive.
It means that you foresee a day when the imminent threat, whatever that may be, diminishes, and you will rebuild. It means that you have taken responsibility for yourself and your family, and that you will not be forced to rely on others. It means that your mind is focused on life itself, not some imaginary life of some reality star that actually has no grasp on reality whatsoever. You have chosen not to be misguided by the lies that the media uses to pacify you.

Preparing yourself is the most optimistic and hopeful thing you can do in a world that would prefer to choose immediate gratification over a firm grasp on reality. Readying yourself to deal with whatever might happen is a joyful act, an expression of gratitude to the Creator, peace made tangible, and the personification of faith itself.

Finally, a quick note to beginners:

As I said in the beginning of this book, please, don't let the thought of all of the preps that you do not yet have bring you down. It's a process, and the most important prep is already in place: your mindset.

Once you know the possibilities, accept them, and begin to prepare, you are already far ahead of most of the neighborhood. You've taken the most important step, the first one, and the rest will come as long as you persevere.

Don't be discouraged by how much you have left to do, instead, be encouraged by how far ahead you are compared to your starting point.

Never underestimate the magnitude of the importance of your state of mind.

A pessimist sees the difficulty in every opportunity; an optimist sees the opportunity in every difficulty.
—Winston Churchill

Happy prepping ~
Daisy

Part VI
PANTRY PRIMER RECIPES AND HOW-TO GUIDES

The recipes and guides here are in order of their appearance in the book. Use them as guidelines and enjoy experimenting based on the items you have available!

RICE MILK

4 servings

Because of the potential toxicity of a heavy consumption of rice (remember how we talked about arsenic?), for long-term usage, you may wish to go with almond milk, which is slightly more involved.

Ingredients:
- 1 cup cooked rice (brown or white)
- 4 cups water
- 1 tsp vanilla (optional)

Directions:
1. Put all of the ingredients into a blender.
2. Process until smooth.
3. For the best flavor, keep cold. Shake well before using.

ALMOND MILK

4 servings

Almond milk has a couple of extra steps—soaking the almonds before processing them in the blender, then straining the finished product through cheesecloth or a flour sack towel.

Ingredients:
- 1 cup almonds
- 4 cups water (plus more for soaking)

Directions:
1. Place almonds in a glass dish. Cover them with water and allow them to soak overnight. You can cover the bowl with a tea towel to keep any contaminants out. Soaking will soften the nuts and make the processing easier and more thorough.
2. Drain the soaking water from the almonds, then place them in your blender with 4 cups of water.
3. Process until smooth.
4. Use a flour sack towel over a clean container to strain the contents of the blender. Don't throw out the almond sludge that you strain out of the milk! This can be dried and added to baked goods and recipes.
5. Like rice milk, almond milk will taste better when cold. Shake well before serving.

POT ROAST

Ingredients:

- Pork or beef roast (plan on 1 pound per person so you have leftovers)
- 1 large onion
- 1 potato per person
- 2 carrots per person
- 2 cloves garlic, whole
- ½ cup water
- ½ cup another liquid, which can be one or a combination of these ingredients: water, beef broth, red wine, apple juice (for pork), cola, strong unsweetened coffee
- Salt and pepper to taste
- 2 Tbsp flour + 2 Tbsp butter for making gravy

Directions:

1. Cut an onion in half and lay it, flat side down, in the bottom of a slow cooker.
2. Cut the carrots and potatoes into bite sized chunks and add them to the bottom of the slow cooker.
3. Place your roast on top of the vegetables, then add the garlic cloves to the top of the roast.
4. Season the roast with salt and pepper.
5. Pour the liquid on top of the roast.
6. Put the lid on the slow cooker and cook this on low for 8–10 hours. The long cooking time means that you can go with a lower quality cut of meat and it will still be fork-tender.
7. At serving time, melt butter in the bottom of a skillet on the stove top. Once the butter is melted, quickly whisk in flour until you have a white creamy concoction with no lumps.
8. Ladle out 1½ cups of the liquid from the slow cooker and pour it into the skillet.

9. Using your whisk, incorporate liquid into the flour and butter mixture. Reduce the heat to low and allow this mixture to gently simmer while you get the meat and vegetables ready to serve. You may need to thin the gravy with an additional half cup of water.

10. Remove the meat and vegetables from the slow cooker, reserving the remaining liquid for your future stew.

11. Slice the meat, reserving a third of it for stew. (If you put all of the meat out, chances are you won't have leftovers, because this is melt-in-your-mouth good.) Serve meat and vegetables with gravy.

LEFTOVER ROAST STEW

"Leftover stew" has been a fixture in our home for years, and the leftovers from a roast make an ideal and delicious foundation for this.

You can modify the recipe to use up whatever leftovers you happen to have on hand. This one presumes that your family didn't inhale every bite of delicious roast and vegetables.

Most of the prep for this stew is done when you are putting away your leftovers. Stirring in the additional liquid before you put this in the refrigerator will allow the flavors to meld until you are ready to make your stew.

Ingredients:
- Leftovers
- Water or broth

Directions:
1. In a large storage container, stir 1–2 cups of water or broth into your reserved cooking liquid. If you have leftover gravy, stir that in, too.
2. Cut the rest of your roast into bite-sized pieces, then add it to the liquid.
3. Add any leftover vegetables to the meat and liquid.
4. Add 1 can of mixed vegetables, including liquid.
5. Put this in the refrigerator for 1–2 days.
6. Heat on the stove top at a simmer for 20 minutes. You can serve this with crusty bread. If there isn't quite enough for a family meal, serve it over wide noodles or rice for a filling, hearty dinner.

PANTRY SPAGHETTI SAUCE

8 servings

Ingredients:
- 1 (28-ounce) can crushed tomatoes
- 3 cloves garlic
- 1 medium onion
- 1 Tbsp sugar
- 1 tsp salt
- 1 tsp thyme
- 1 tsp oregano
- 1 Tbsp basil
- Black pepper to taste
- Pinch of paprika (smoked Hungarian, if you can find it)
- 2 Tbsp extra-virgin olive oil
- Optional: ½ cup fresh sliced mushrooms and ½ cup diced bell pepper
- Optional: 1 pound ground beef
- Fresh grated Parmesan for the top

Directions:
1. In a food processor, place a quarter cup of the crushed tomatoes, along with the garlic, onion, sugar, spices, and bell peppers if you're using them. Process until pureed.
2. Pour the rest of the crushed tomatoes, the pureed mixture, and the optional mushrooms into a stockpot.
3. If you want to add meat, stir in your ground meat or meatballs now too.
4. Simmer on a low heat for about 3 hours. (You can cook it for longer if you want to, or you can cook this all day on low in the slow cooker.) Drizzle with olive oil and allow it to cook for another 15 minutes.
5. Serve over pasta, topped with Parmesan.

SPAGHETTI PIE

4 servings

This is a great way to make the most of your spaghetti dinner leftovers.

Ingredients:
- 1–2 eggs
- 1 cup cottage cheese
- 1 tsp garlic powder
- ¼ cup fresh-grated Parmesan cheese, plus additional for the top
- 1 serving of cooked pasta for each family member
- Leftover spaghetti with meat sauce
- Optional: extra chopped fresh vegetables like tomato, mushroom, bell pepper, spinach, and onion
- ½ cup toasted bread crumbs

Directions:
1. Preheat the oven to 350°F.
2. In a large bowl, beat the eggs and cottage cheese with garlic powder and Parmesan cheese. Alternatively, you can also blend this together in a food processor.
3. Stir in cooked pasta until it is well coated.
4. Stir in leftover spaghetti sauce and optional chopped vegetables.
5. Pour the mixture into a greased ovenproof pie plate or skillet. (I use my cast-iron frying pan for this.)
6. Cover with foil and bake for 30 minutes in your preheated oven.
7. Combine extra Parmesan and toasted breadcrumbs for the topping.
8. After the 30 minutes, increase heat to 425°F. Remove foil, top with additional Parmesan and toasted breadcrumbs, and bake for 15 more minutes, until the top is lightly crisped.
9. Remove the pie from the oven and allow it to set for 15 minutes before slicing.

SLOW COOKER HAM AND POTATOES

4 servings

Ingredients:

- 2 Tbsp butter for the sides and bottom of the slow cooker
- Potatoes, thinly sliced (Count on 2 medium potatoes per family member)
- 1 large onion, minced
- 2 cloves garlic, minced
- Salt and pepper to taste
- Optional: Favorite herbs and spices (We like thyme and paprika in this dish)
- ½ cup water
- Diced or sliced ham (this is the other half of the ham you bought for sandwiches)
- ½ cup milk
- 1 cup cottage cheese, pureed

Directions:

1. Coat the sides of the slow cooker with butter.
2. Add potatoes, onion, garlic, salt, pepper, and optional seasonings if you're using them, and water to the slow cooker. Stir to combine.
3. Top with ham.
4. Put the lid on and cook on low for 4–6 hours.
5. Combine the milk and pureed cottage cheese. Then remove the lid from the slow cooker and gently stir the mixture in, being careful not to break up the potatoes too much.
6. Replace the lid and continue to cook on low for another 2 hours, then enjoy.

LEFTOVER POTATO AND HAM SOUP

6 servings

Ingredients:

- 2–3 cups of leftover Slow Cooker Ham and Potatoes
- 1 cup milk
- 2 cups water

Directions:

1. Once you're finished with your potato and ham dinner, add 1 cup of milk and 2 cups of water to the leftovers before refrigerating.
2. When you're ready to make your soup, use a potato masher to break up the potatoes well. If you want, you can run the entire batch through the food processor, but my family prefers the chunks of meat and potatoes.
3. Stir the soup together well once the potatoes have been mashed up.
4. Heat this up, bringing it to a simmer. If it's too thick, you can add more milk or water. (Milk will make it richer, but if your supplies are limited, water will be fine.)
5. Top the soup like you would a baked potato, with Greek yogurt or sour cream, shredded cheese, and chives.

HOMEMADE YOGURT

2 servings

Ingredients:
- 2 cups milk
- ½ cup yogurt with active cultures (your starter)

Directions:
1. Heat the milk to 165–185°F. (use a candy thermometer—or, if you don't have one, wait until you are starting to see some bubbles rising but the milk is not yet boiling).
2. Remove the milk from the heat and allow it to drop to 105–110°F.
3. Meanwhile, put hot water in your thermos to warm it up.
4. Gently stir in the starter. You want it to be well combined, but don't use anything crazy like an immersion blender. Remember, the good bacteria that create the yogurt are alive, so don't kill them with too much heat or overly vigorous mixing. Just a whisk will do.
5. Pour the hot water out of the thermos.
6. Immediately place the mixture into the thermos that has been warmed with hot water and put the lid on.
7. Keep the thermos cozily wrapped in towels overnight (8–24 hours). It has to stay warm. When we lived in an off-grid cabin, I tucked the wrapped thermos behind the woodstove at night to keep it at a warm enough temperature.
8. Get up and enjoy some delicious, rich, thick yogurt.

Tips:
- The longer you leave it, the thicker and more tart your yogurt will be. If you intend to use it in place of sour cream, leave it longer.
- If you are using raw milk, heat it up only to 160°F.
- Always save a little of your yogurt to be a starter for the next batch. I like to put a half cup in the fridge, stored separately so it doesn't accidentally get eaten.

HOMEMADE YOGURT CHEESE

2 servings

Yogurt cheese isn't actually cheese, but it can be used in place of cream cheese in many different recipes or applications. Yogurt cheese is simply yogurt with the whey strained out.

Ingredients:
- 1 cup unflavored yogurt

Directions:
1. Line a sieve with a piece of cheesecloth or a flour sack towel. Place it over a large bowl.
2. Scoop one cup of plain yogurt onto the fabric.
3. Cover the whole thing and place it in the refrigerator for a minimum of 2 hours. The longer you allow it to drain, the thicker the end consistency will be. When it's done, transfer your cheese to a bowl and season it up.

For sweet cheese:
This makes a delicious spread for bagels or toast, and a nice quick topping for cupcakes.
   Stir in any combination of the following:
- 1 Tbsp honey or sugar
- Cinnamon
- Nutmeg
- Allspice
- ½ tsp vanilla extract

For savory cheese:
This makes a tasty spread for sandwiches or filling for stuffed vegetables or chicken breasts.
   Stir in any combination of the following to taste:
- Salt
- Pepper

- Garlic
- Onion
- Horseradish
- Cayenne pepper
- Thyme
- Basil
- Chives
- Finely chopped sun-dried tomatoes and Mediterranean spices like oregano and basil

HOMEMADE COTTAGE CHEESE

4 servings

The thing that shocked me the most the first time I made my own cottage cheese was that I made this creamy deliciousness with only 3 simple ingredients.

This is, for real, the easiest thing that I've ever made. Even better, it's far less expensive than purchasing a ready-made container of organic cottage cheese.

Ingredients:
- 2½ cups 2% milk or raw milk
- ¼ cup white vinegar
- Dash of salt (optional)

Directions:
1. In a large saucepan, bring the milk almost to a boil. As soon as bubbles begin to rise to the top, remove the saucepan from the heat.
2. Immediately stir in the white vinegar and the salt (if using). The milk will begin to curdle right away.
3. Allow the mixture to cool completely—about 1 hour at room temperature. (The longer you leave it to cool, the more curds you will have. You can even put it in the fridge overnight before draining.)
4. Using a mesh strainer, separate the curds and the whey. (Hints of Little Miss Muffet!) The result will be a delicious, light, and fluffy cottage cheese. This recipe falls just short of 1 cup of cottage cheese and just over a cup and a half of whey. If the flavor is a bit sour (more common with pasteurized milk and very rare with raw milk) you can rinse the curds gently under running water, then drain again.

Don't throw out your whey!

Here are some uses for it:

- Substitute for water or milk in baking
- Use instead of water when cooking rice or pasta
- Use it for smoothies
- Use it in oatmeal or other porridge

ROASTED CHICKEN

6 servings

This is a very simple meal, but classic and delicious enough to serve to guests.

Ingredients:
- 5–6 pound whole chicken
- 1 head of garlic
- 1 medium onion, peeled
- Salt, pepper, and herbs to taste

Directions:
1. Preheat your oven to 425°F.
2. Rinse the chicken inside and out under running water. (Be sure to wash out your sink with a bleach solution afterwards to keep your kitchen free of bacteria that could cause foodborne illness.)
3. If there is a package of "giblets and guts" inside your chicken, remove it. You can use this later for gravy, add it to your homemade stock, or cook it up for the pets. Keep in mind that liver will give an off-flavor to your stock.
4. Insert the entire head of garlic into the cavity of the chicken. You don't have to peel the garlic first—just put the entire head in there for a rich-flavored meat.
5. Cut the onion in half and place it, cut side down, in the roasting pan. This will keep the chicken raised up out of the drippings. If you are using a roasting pan with a rack, you can put the onion in the cavity with the garlic.
6. Sprinkle the chicken liberally with salt, pepper, and herbs of your choice.
7. Place this in the oven, uncovered, for about an hour and a half. Using a meat thermometer in the thickest part of the breast, check to see if it is done. The temperature should be 180°F. If you don't have a meat thermometer, gently give the leg a twist.

When the chicken is completely cooked, the leg should separate very easily under the lightest pressure.

8. Remove the chicken from the roasting pan and allow it to rest for 15 minutes at room temperature.

9. Carve the chicken, discarding the garlic and onion from the cavity. Put aside the skin for use in your broth, later.

HOW TO MAKE GRAVY

This basic guide will work to make any type of gravy: beef, pork, poultry, etc.

Ingredients:

- Pan drippings
- 2 Tbsp flour
- 1–2 cups water or broth
- Salt and pepper to taste

Directions:

1. Add hot drippings to a saucepan and turn the heat on your stove to medium.
2. When the drippings are hot enough that a tiny bit of water splashed in with your fingertips sizzles on contact, use a whisk to mix in the flour. Whisk vigorously until the flour and fat are completely incorporated with no lumps. You should end up with a smooth, creamy-looking mixture. (This is called a roux.)
3. Stir in the water or broth. Broth gives a slightly richer flavor, but gravy made with water is still delicious and much more frugal. Using the whisk, mix the roux and water thoroughly. Season as desired.
4. Cook, whisking almost continuously, for 3–5 minutes until your gravy reaches a uniform consistency and the desired thickness. If it is too thick, whisk in more liquid, half a cup at a time.
5. Keep warm over the lowest heat your stove allows.

CHICKEN BROTH

Don't throw out that chicken carcass! You can get more bang for your poultry buck by making broth with it. Use this same process for turkey broth.

1. After dinner, remove most of the meat from the bones and place it in the refrigerator. You'll be left with a rather desolate-looking carcass.

2. Put that in your slow cooker along with the reserved skin, neck, and giblets (if you didn't use those for gravy). Add some veggies like carrots, peppers, and celery. Add a couple of tablespoons of salt, a head of garlic, and 4–6 onions. (Note: there's no need to peel the vegetables as long as they are organic—just wash them well.)

3. Fill the slow cooker with water and add your favorite spices (not sage, if you intend to preserve the broth—it tastes terrible when canned or frozen). I like to use whole peppercorns, salt, oregano, and bay leaves.

4. Put the slow cooker on low for 12–14 hours and let it simmer undisturbed overnight.

5. The next day, strain the contents of the slow cooker into a large container—I use a big soup pot and a metal colander.

6. After allowing the bones to cool, remove any meat that you would like to add to your soup. Take all of the meat that you put in the refrigerator the night before and cut it into bite-sized pieces. I like a mixture of light meat and dark meat for this purpose. Also cut up the meat you removed from the slow cooker.

Canning the broth

(See the canning instructions in Part V of this book for specific instructions on sanitizing jars, pressure canning, and adjusting for altitude.)

1. Place approximately 1 cup of meat in each of your sanitized jars. If you're only canning the broth, skip this step.

2. Add 1–2 cloves of garlic to the jars.

3. You will have a rich, dark beautiful stock from the overnight slow cooker project. Ladle this into the jars over your cut-up poultry and garlic. Leave 1 inch of headspace at the top of the jars. If you run out of broth, top it up with water—don't worry, your broth will still be very flavorful.

4. Wipe the lip of your jars with a cloth dipped in white vinegar. Place the lids on and process them in your pressure canner for 90 minutes at 10 pounds of pressure, being sure to adjust for altitude.

Your result will be a deep golden, rich, meaty soup. This is an excellent base for poultry and dumplings, as well as any type of broth-based soup.

Freezing the broth

1. Allow your broth to cool completely. Use a heavy-duty freezer bag (I like the kind with the actual zipper).

2. If you are adding meat to the broth, place the desired amount in the bottom of the freezer bag. If you aren't adding the meat, skip this step.

3. Ladle the cooled broth into the bag, leaving 2 inches of headspace at the top.

4. Seal the bag securely, then lay it flat on a cookie sheet. Repeat this process until all of the broth is bagged up.

5. Freeze the broth flat overnight. After that, it should be frozen solid. Label the bags with a permanent marker, including the date. The flat bags of broth can be stacked in the freezer for about 6 months.

BAKED BROWN RICE

6 servings

Lots of people complain that brown rice is tricky to cook. Take it off the stovetop and cook it in the oven for absolutely perfect rice every time. For efficiency, bake your rice when you are cooking something else in the oven.

Ingredients:
- 1½ cups brown rice
- 2½ cups water, broth, or stock
- 1 Tbsp butter or olive oil
- Salt, pepper, and herbs to taste
- Optional: dried sweetened cranberries

Directions:
1. Preheat the oven to 400°F.
2. On the stovetop, bring rice, liquid, seasonings, cranberries (if you're using them), and fat to a boil in an oven-safe pot.
3. Immediately put the lid on it, remove it from the stovetop, and place it in the oven.
4. Bake for 1 hour. Do not remove the lid during the cooking time.
5. Fluff the rice with a fork and serve immediately.Leftover rice can be refrigerated and used in a casserole or stir-fry.

CHICKEN FRIED RICE

This is a great way to extend a single serving of meat to provide dinner for an entire family. Feel free to get creative and use other types of meat and additional veggies. If the vegetables are pre-cooked, add them at the very end, giving them just enough time in the skillet to get warmed up.

Ingredients:

- 1 Tbsp cooking oil (I like sunflower or organic canola—oil must stand up to high-heat cooking methods)
- 1–2 eggs (Use 1 egg per 2 cups of rice, not to exceed two eggs)
- 2 cloves garlic, minced
- 1 small onion, minced
- 1 cup cooked chicken (or other meat), cut into bite-sized pieces
- $\frac{1}{4}$ cup shredded carrot
- 1 tsp powdered ginger
- 2 Tbsp soy sauce
- 1 tsp Asian fish sauce (optional, but it adds a lot of depth and does not impart a "fishy" flavor)
- $\frac{1}{2}$–1 cup cooked rice per person
- 1 cup frozen green peas
- Green onions and chili peppers for topping

Directions:

1. In a large skillet or wok, heat cooking oil over a medium heat.
2. Crack eggs and mix them in a bowl with a whisk. Reserve them for later in the cooking process.
3. Add garlic, onion, and chicken to your heated skillet. Stir fry for a few minutes until everything is lightly golden.
4. Add carrots and stir fry for another minute or two.
5. Add eggs and let them cook for 1 minute without stirring so they get a little bit firm. Then, stir constantly for a couple of

minutes so that they break up as they're cooking, leaving only tiny pieces of egg throughout the mixture of ingredients.

6. Sprinkle with ginger, then stir in soy sauce and optional fish sauce.
7. Increase heat to high, then stir in rice and peas.
8. Stirring constantly, cook until everything is heated through. Serve topped with chopped green onion and optional dried crushed chili peppers.

Tip: For a Thai-twist, add ¼ cup of peanut butter and 1 tsp of cilantro during step 6.

CHILI

8 servings

Chili is a family favorite in our house. One of my favorite things about it is that it can be easily made from food storage items. Here's a version that is largely from the pantry. You can use a slow cooker or simmer it on low on the stovetop. If necessary, it can be put together quickly and just cooked until the ingredients are done, but it won't be nearly as flavorful and delicious.

Ingredients:

- Tomatoes: Use any combination of the following, equaling 3 large cans: crushed tomatoes, diced tomatoes, tomato-vegetable juice
- 1 cup beer or red wine (optional, but delicious if you are using a slow cooker)
- 1–3 Tbsp chili powder
- 1 tsp cumin powder
- 1 Tbsp brown sugar
- 2 cans of beans (pinto, kidney, black)—do not drain
- 4 cloves minced garlic
- 1 diced bell pepper
- 1 diced onion
- 1 pound ground meat (whatever you have on hand: beef, turkey, venison, pork)

Slow Cooker Directions:

1. Stir together tomato products, alcohol, and spices until well combined.
2. Add beans with their liquid, stirring to combine.
3. Add garlic, peppers, and onions, stirring to combine.
4. Add ground meat. Stir gently to combine it into the mixture in your slow cooker.

5. Set the slow cooker on low and cook for 8–10 hours, or on high and cook for 4–5 hours. (It's best when cooked all day on low.)

Stovetop Directions:
1. In a skillet, brown meat, garlic, and onions until the meat is cooked—about 5 minutes.
2. Meanwhile, in a large pot, combine tomato products, beans, peppers, and spices.
3. Add cooked meat, garlic, and onions to the large pot.
4. Bring the mixture to a low boil, then reduce heat.
5. Simmer, covered, for 2–3 hours.

BERNADINE'S "CHILI MAC"

8 servings

If you have leftover chili, but not quite enough to make a meal for everyone, try this classic dish I adapted from a recipe created by my honorary childhood aunt, a lovely lady who just turned 100 years old and ran a school cafeteria for much of her adult life, back when the food served there was made from scratch, from real ingredients, and on a strict budget.

Don't let the name fool you, there's no macaroni in sight, making this safe for those on a gluten-free diet. (If you absolutely insist, you *can* use macaroni instead of rice.) Bernadine created this recipe when the kids at her school were expecting Chili Mac but her food delivery only contained rice and no pasta. They loved it so much that she made it again and again and lots of them went on to make Bernadine's Chili Mac (with rice) for their own families. (My mom included.)

Ingredients:
- Butter for the baking dish
- 2–4 cups leftover chili
- 4–6 cups cooked rice (brown or white will work)
- 1 cup shredded cheddar cheese

Directions:
1. Preheat the oven to 400°F.
2. Grease the bottom and sides of a glass baking dish.
3. In a large mixing bowl, stir together the chili and the rice.
4. Pour the chili and rice mixture into the baking dish and cover it tightly with foil.
5. Bake for 30 minutes.
6. After 30 minutes, remove the foil and top the casserole with shredded cheese.
7. Return it to the oven for another 5 minutes, or until cheese is melted and bubbly.
8. Allow the dish to cool for 5 minutes before serving.

HAYSTACK COOKIES

18 cookies

Ingredients:

- ¾ cup sugar
- ¾ cup milk
- 5 tsp cocoa
- 1 Tbsp vanilla extract
- 1 cup natural peanut butter
- 3 cups oatmeal

Directions:

1. Line a large baking sheet with waxed paper.
2. In a sauce pan, stir together all of the ingredients except for the peanut butter and the oatmeal.
3. Heat the saucepan until these ingredients are combined, then add peanut butter, stirring constantly until boiling gently.
4. Boil for one minute, stirring intermittently.
5. Remove from heat and pour into a bowl containing the oatmeal.
6. Stir to combine, working quickly before the mixture can solidify.
7. Make the cookies by placing large spoonsfuls of the mixture onto the paper-lined baking sheet. Press them down gently with the back of the spoon.
8. Alternatively, use your hand to roll balls of the mixture and then press down—this will make the resulting cookies a bit rounder if you prefer a tidier looking cookie. (Be careful, though, the mixture is hot—that whole boiling thing, you know!)
9. Place the cookie sheet in the refrigerator overnight, uncovered, to allow cookies to become solid.
10. Store in an airtight container in cool conditions—keep them in the fridge if the weather is warm. Reuse the waxed paper by placing it in between the layers of cookies.

COOKING BEANS FROM SCRATCH

8 servings

Do you know what to do with all of those bags of beans? It's silly to buy them if you don't learn how to prepare them. As cheap as they are, they do your budget little good sitting there in storage containers.

There are minor differences in soaking and cooking times with different types of beans, but if you follow these basic directions, you'll be successful. The obvious, common sense difference is that smaller beans require a shorter cooking time than larger beans.

Prepping the beans for cooking:
1. Start with one pound of dried beans. Our favorites are pinto beans and navy beans.
2. Pour them into a bowl and pick through them, discarding any beans that are dry and shriveled, and any little stones or twigs.
3. Using a large colander, rinse the beans well under running water.
4. Place your beans in a large stockpot. Cover them with water by 3–4 inches.
5. Turn the stove on high and bring the beans to a boil. Turn off the heat immediately, and cover them to soak. You can soak them overnight, or a minimum of 4 hours.
6. Drain the beans using a colander, then rinse them well under running water.

Cooking directions:
1. Return the soaked beans to the stockpot.
2. Cover them with 3 cups of water per cup of beans.
3. If you want, you can also add some meat at this point. Salt pork, ham, and bacon are popular choices. If you aren't using meat, add a tablespoon of vegetable oil. The fat not only adds flavor but keeps the beans from foaming.

4. You can also add onions, garlic, and herbs to the beans now. Don't add anything acidic until they are fully cooked.
5. Bring the beans to a boil, then immediately reduce the heat to keep them at a simmer.
6. Stir occasionally to be sure the beans aren't sticking. The beans must always stay covered with water. You may need to add water during the cooking process.
7. Simmer for 2–3 hours. To test whether they are done, remove a bean from the pot and let it cool. Taste it—it should be tender, but not mushy. There are lots of variables that will affect how long they take to cook—weather conditions, altitude, and the age of the beans can affect cooking times.
8. When they're done, you can leave them in the cooking liquid or drain them, based on personal preferences. (I grew up down south, where my family always enjoyed them in the "bean broth.")

Serve your cooked beans as a dish on their own or use one of the following variations.

PORK AND BEANS

10 servings

You can start this recipe with home-cooked beans or canned beans. It can be made on the stovetop or baked in the oven.

Ingredients:

- ½ cup bean broth (If you're using canned beans, use this liquid from the can)
- 6 ounce can of tomato paste
- 2 Tbsp brown sugar
- 1 tsp chili powder
- 1 tsp onion powder
- 1 tsp garlic powder
- Salt and pepper to taste
- 6 cups cooked beans
- 1 cup diced smoked pork or ham, or ½ pound diced bacon

Directions:

1. In a large mixing bowl, combine bean broth, tomato paste, sugar, and spices until well blended.
2. Stir in beans and pork.
3. If you are cooking this on the stovetop, put the mixture into a pot and bring it to a simmer. Put the lid on and cook it on low for 30 minutes.
4. If you are cooking it in the oven, preheat it to 375°F. Grease a baking dish with cooking oil or butter, then pour in the mixture. Cover it with foil and bake for 45 minutes.

MEXICAN BEANS AND RICE

4 servings

Ingredients:
- 1 Tbsp cooking oil
- ¼ cup diced onion and/or ¼ cup of diced bell peppers (optional)
- ½ cup bean broth
- 2 Tbsp tomato paste
- 1 Tbsp chili powder
- 1 tsp cumin
- 1 tsp garlic powder
- 1 tsp onion powder
- Salt and pepper to taste
- 2 cups cooked rice
- 2 cups cooked beans (You can use leftover pork and beans for this, too)

Directions:
1. In a large skillet, heat cooking oil.
2. Add onions and bell peppers, if you're using them, and sauté lightly over medium heat.
3. Stir in bean broth, tomato paste, and spices.
4. Stir in rice, then when it is combined, gently stir in beans, taking care not to break them up when mixing them in.
5. Reduce the heat, cover, and cook for 15–20 minutes on low. If you need to, add ¼ cup of water to keep the mixture from sticking.

Serve topped with cheese, sour cream, and/or salsa.

CORNBREAD

8 servings

This quick bread was a staple when I was growing up. My dad, who was a child of the Great Depression, loved nothing more than a big slice of cornbread topped with pinto beans in their own broth. Unless perhaps it was cornbread broken up into a glass of buttermilk and eaten with a spoon, a dish I never personally enjoyed.

Some people like their cornbread sweet, while others don't like the addition of any sugar or honey. This ingredient is entirely optional. This recipe is naturally gluten-free, so it doesn't rise much. If you want a fluffy cornbread, replace half of the cornmeal with flour. Maybe I'm a traditionalist, but in my humble opinion, cornbread is at its best when cooked in a cast-iron skillet.

Ingredients:
- 1 Tbsp white vinegar
- 1½ cups milk
- 4 Tbsp butter or cooking oil + extra for greasing your skillet
- 2 cups cornmeal
- 1 tsp salt
- 1 tsp baking soda
- 2 tsp baking powder
- 1 egg
- 4 Tbsp brown sugar or honey (optional)

Directions:
1. Preheat the oven to 400°F.
2. In a bowl, combine white vinegar and milk and set it aside for at least 5 minutes to allow it to sour.
3. Grease the skillet well with oil or butter.
4. Meanwhile, in a large mixing bowl, combine all of the dry ingredients with a whisk, including sugar if you are using it.

5. Add eggs and honey (if you're using it) to the sour milk. Whisk until well-combined.
6. Stir the wet ingredients into the dry ingredients until they are just combined.
7. Pour this mixture into the cast-iron skillet.
8. Bake the cornbread for about 20 minutes. The top should be golden brown and crispy, and a toothpick inserted in the middle should come out clean.

Variations:

Mexican cornbread: Add 1 cup of cooked corn, a couple of diced jalapeños, and a cup of shredded cheese to the batter. Reduce the sweetener by half.

Blueberry cornbread: Add one cup of fresh, frozen, or rehydrated blueberries to the cornbread batter. Sugar and honey should definitely be used when making blueberry cornbread.

CHICKEN AND DUMPLINGS

6 servings

Ingredients:

- 2 cups flour (You can use a gluten-free flour blend) + extra for dusting the counter and the rolling pin
- Salt, pepper, and parsley to taste
- 1 cup water
- 1 egg
- 4–6 cups chicken broth with meat

Directions:

1. In a large mixing bowl, combine flour and seasonings. Stir in water and egg, combining well. You will have a dry, crumbly mixture.
2. Squeeze the dough by handfuls and put it on a counter that has been dusted with flour.
3. Roll out the dough until it is flat, about ¼-inch thick.
4. Using a pizza cutter or a sharp knife, cut the dough into strips or squares, according to your preference. Allow it to dry on the counter for up to 2 hours.
5. When it's time for dinner, bring broth and chicken to a hard boil on the stovetop, using a high heat.
6. Drop the dumplings in, being careful not to splash yourself with the hot liquid.
7. When the dumplings rise to the top, they are done. To be certain, dip out one dumpling and cut it in half to let it cool. Taste it to make sure it isn't still doughy inside. If it needs more cooking time, return the other half to the pot and cook it for a few more minutes.
8. Serve dumplings and broth piping hot.

SHEPHERD'S PIE

6 servings

This is a great way to use up mashed potatoes and leftover vegetables. This is another food that cooks up wonderfully in a cast-iron skillet.

Ingredients:
- 1 tsp olive oil
- 2 cloves garlic, minced
- ½ onion, minced
- 1 pound ground meat (any kind will work—the traditional is lamb, but we often use beef, pork, or turkey)
- ½ cup mushrooms, finely chopped
- Salt and pepper to taste
- 2–3 cups drained cooked vegetables, any combination (we like corn, peas, and carrots)
- 3 cups mashed potatoes
- 2 Tbsp butter, optional

Directions:
1. On the stovetop, heat cooking oil in the cast iron skillet over a medium heat. Lightly sauté garlic, mushrooms, and onion.
2. Meanwhile, preheat the oven to 400°F.
3. Add the ground meat to the skillet and brown it thoroughly.
4. Season the meat mixture with salt and pepper.
5. Remove the skillet from the heat, then stir in the cooked veggies.
6. Press the mixture into the skillet with the back of a spatula.
7. Top it with mashed potatoes. If you want, you can add a little butter to the top of the potatoes.
8. Bake this in the oven for 35 minutes or until the top of the potatoes is very lightly golden brown and crisp.
9. Remove the casserole from the oven and allow it to rest for 10 minutes. Slice it into triangles like a pie and serve.

POWER OUTAGE FOOD GUIDE

I like to keep some foods on hand that require no cooking or heating. In the event of a power outage, sometimes it's nice to have no-hassle foods so that you don't have to heat up the house in the summer with a fire or go outside in a raging storm to use an off-grid cooking method.

These foods aren't quite as nutritious and non-processed as the things I normally serve. Following are some "recipes" for power outage food. Okay, "recipe" is a stretch—perhaps just some "tasty combinations." You can improve the nutritional value by opting for organic, less processed versions wherever possible.

No-Power Nachos
Layer organic tortilla chips with canned cheese sauce, salsa, and canned jalapenos.

S'mores
Top graham crackers with Nutella (or another healthier chocolate-nut spread) and marshmallow fluff.

Wraps
Fill soft tortillas with canned meat, a touch of mustard or mayo, and veggies from the fridge.

No-cook Soft Tacos
Fill soft tortillas with canned meat (we use our home-canned chicken or taco meat for this), salsa, and canned cheese sauce.

Main Dish Tuna Salad
Combine a can of tuna, a can of white beans, chopped onion, chopped peppers, and chopped black olives (veggies are optional). Top with Italian dressing mixed with Dijon mustard to taste.

Pudding Cones

Drain canned fruit of choice and stir it into vanilla pudding. Serve in ice cream cones for a kid-friendly treat. (We do this with yogurt also.)

Mexican Bean Salad

Combine 1 can of black beans, drained and rinsed, with 1 can of organic corn, drained. For the dressing, mix 1/2 jar of salsa; 1/2 tsp each of chili powder, onion powder, and garlic powder; 3 Tbsp of lemon juice. Toss well. Serve as a salad, in a soft tortilla, or mixed with a pouch of precooked rice.

ACKNOWLEDGMENTS

This book is dedicated to the readers who comment, whether good or bad, on my website. It is for the people who review my books, whether those reviews are positive or negative. Your feedback is my guide: it tells me what you want to learn, it tells me what you like and dislike about my books, and it helps me to be a better writer. Without your input, this book would not be possible. Thank you.

It is also, as always, dedicated to my daughters, C and R, who tirelessly taste-test recipes and who gracefully tolerate having an eccentric mom. Thanks for listening to ideas, brainstorming, reading, designing, encouraging, and flat-out telling me when something is lame, even if I think it sounds like the world's most fantastic, revolutionary idea at the time. I love you two more than anything in this world or beyond and it is YOU who have been my motivation to succeed. I wouldn't be where I am today without you marvelous young women.

As always, this book is also dedicated to the memory of my dad, who inspired me in his last days by reminding me that writers don't just talk about writing. Writers write. This book is also dedicated to my mom, who loves seeing my books in print and who pushed me to excel every single day when I was young.

ABOUT THE AUTHOR

Daisy Luther is an author and blogger who lives in the mountains in the eastern US. For now, anyway. She is the author of *The Prepper's Water Survival Guide* and *The Prepper's Canning Guide*, as well as numerous self-published titles that you can find in her online bookstore on her website.

Her blog is **TheOrganicPrepper.com**. Daisy uses her background in alternative journalism to provide a unique perspective on subjects such as current events, preparedness, health, and personal liberty. Daisy's articles are widely republished throughout alternative media and she has been interviewed on many mainstream outlets.

She is the coffee-swigging, gun-toting mama of two wonderful, sensible, talented daughters and 4 furry beasts.

INDEX